MAKE MONEY

IN

SHORT-SALE FORECLOSURES

MAKE MONEY

IN

SHORT-SALE
FORECLOSURES

How to Bypass
Owners and Buy Directly
from Lenders

CHANTAL HOWELL CAREY
BILL CAREY

WILEY

John Wiley & Sons, Inc.

Published by John Wiley & Sons, Inc., Hoboken, New Jersey.
Published simultaneously in Canada.

For general information on our other products and services or for technical support, please contact our Customer Care Department within the United States at (800) 762-2974, outside the United States at (317) 572-3993 or fax (317) 572-4002.

Wiley also publishes its books in a variety of electronic formats. Some content that appears in print may not be available in electronic books. For more information about Wiley products, visit our Web site at www.wiley.com.

Library of Congress Cataloging-in-Publication Data:
Howell Carey, Chantal.
    Make money in short-sale foreclosures: how to bypass owners and buy directly from lenders / Chantal Howell Carey, Bill Carey.
        p. cm.
    Includes index.
    ISBN-13: 978-0-471-76084-9 (cloth)
    ISBN-10: 0-471-76084-6 (cloth)
        1. Real estate investment—United States. 2. Foreclosure—United States. 3. House buying—United States. 4. Real property—Purchasing—United States. I. Carey, Bill, 1951- II. Title.
HD255.H659   2006
332.63'24—dc22   2005029724

Printed in the United States of America.

10 9 8 7 6 5 4 3 2 1

With love to all our family, friends, and dedicated students!
May you always have more blessings than you need!

CONTENTS

PREFACE

The national foreclosure rate continues to increase. Today more than two of every one hundred mortgage loans are in the foreclosure process. The numbers according to the Mortgage Bankers Association say 550,000 to 650,000 mortgages are either delinquent or in foreclosure. In the Dallas-Fort Worth metropolitan area alone foreclosures have increased 93 percent since 1999.

We believe one of the best opportunities in the last 30 years to make money in foreclosures is happening for the smart real estate investor. Over the next five years people who invest in real estate foreclosures are going to make tens of thousands of dollars.

As real estate markets cool over the next 12 to 18 months, the number of loans that are delinquent or in foreclosure will increase. Because of the aggressive lending practices of real estate lenders both in purchasing and refinancing over the last three years, many properties are overfinanced.

This means that borrowers/owners have greatly reduced equity positions. When they get behind in their mortgage payments, their loan becomes a nonperforming loan. When this happens, their lenders are going to get stuck with the properties. Lenders will have to develop strategies to quickly liquidate the nonperforming loans in their loan portfolios. Otherwise, they will face the wrath of the Federal Reserve and the banking regulators. They will also not be fulfilling their loan portfolio requirements for their investors.

Waiting for the traditional foreclosure sale or taking back properties that do not sell at the foreclosure sale will not help the lender's balance sheet. The short-sale market, with lenders selling properties to investors before the foreclosure sale for a wholesale price, will increase dramatically.

In 2003 and 2004, mortgage statistics said that one out of 20 foreclosures resulted in a lender short-sale. This is 5 percent of the foreclosure market. In 2006 and 2007 it has been estimated that 1 out of 10 foreclosures will result in a lender short-sale. Although this will be only 10 percent of the foreclosure market, it will be a 100 percent increase in the short-sale market!

Short-Sale Foreclosures

Most foreclosure books teach an investor how to buy the equity of an owner in foreclosure. But what if the owner has little or no equity for an investor to buy? The owner having little or no equity could be for several reasons. Property in the area may not have appreciated very much. The owner may have made little or no down payment when they bought the property. The property could be in disrepair. Maybe the owner got in financial trouble soon after buying or refinancing the property. Typically, most investors walk away from these little or no equity opportunities. We offer the sophisticated investor a way to turn these opportunities into profits.

Make Money in Short-Sale Foreclosures: How to Bypass Owners and Buy Directly from Lenders teaches you how to have the mortgage lender with a nonperforming loan accept less than the amount of the loan balance for the loan payoff. You are literally reducing or, in technical terms, cramming down the amount the lender receives and buying the property for less than the loan amount. This is buying real estate for a short-sale or wholesale price.

Let's look at an example. Let's say a borrower is three months behind on their $1,200 monthly mortgage payment. The amount outstanding on their loan is $200,000, and the lender is about to foreclose. The lender would like to receive the $200,000 loan balance plus $3,600 for the three back payments.

Loan Balance	$200,000
Back Payments	+$3,600
Lender Desired Payoff	$203,600

Let's say the property is worth $210,000. The owner has little or no equity in the property.

Property Value	$210,000
Lender Desired Payoff	−$203,600
Owner's Equity	$6,400

Subtracting an additional $14,000 to $16,000 in closing costs (real estate commissions, escrow fees, attorney's fees, and title insurance) if the owner were to sell the property would leave the owner having to put money into the deal!

Owner's Equity	$6,400
Closing Costs	$16,000
Additional Owner Money	($9,600)

As a typical real estate investor it appears that there is no way for you to make money in this situation. But you are not a typical real estate investor. This is where the knowledge *you* have gained from *Make Money in Short-Sale Foreclosures: How to Bypass Owners and Buy Directly from Lenders* allows *you* to make money.

Your competition thinks there is no way to make money on this deal, but *you* know there is a way to make money on this deal. (Actually, you have no competition because 90 to 95 percent of your competition has already walked away.) You will do a short-sale deal.

We show you how to negotiate with the lender so that the lender will accept a reduced or short-sale loan payoff. Let's say you offer the lender $169,000 for the property. When the lender accepts your offer, you have an instant $41,000 equity position!

Property Value	$210,000
Negotiated Lender Payoff	−$169,000
Your Equity	$41,000

Negotiating with the Lender

Why would the lender accept your $169,000 loan payoff offer? Because, ultimately it is in the lender's best interest to do so! The sooner the lender gets the nonperforming asset off their books, the better for the lender. Let's look at the numbers from the lender's perspective.

If the lender goes through the foreclosure process and no one bids at the foreclosure sale because it looks like there is no equity in the property, the lender still has all the foreclosure costs. The initial lender costs include posting a notice of foreclosure and advertising the foreclosure sale. The lender will next have to pay attorney's fees and trustee's fees. Then there is the actual foreclosure sale expense they will have to pay. Also the lender will have to pay for title insurance. The list goes on. The total of lender foreclosure expenses could easily be $3,000 to $4,000.

After the lender takes back the property, they have additional expenses. The lender must pay for repairs and fix-up costs, ongoing maintenance, hazard insurance, property taxes, and human resources costs. Let's call these costs *holding costs*. Again, the list goes on. This could easily amount to another $5,000 to $6,000.

And finally, the lender will have to put the property on the market for sale. The lender will have the closing costs and real estate commissions to pay in the same range as the seller pays. This is an additional $14,000 to $16,000!

The lender was hoping to receive $203,600. Assume they received this amount when they finally sell the property. What would the lender net after all costs?

Lender Payoff	$203,600
Foreclosure Costs	$4,000
Holding Costs	$6,000
Closing Costs	−$16,000
Lender's Net	$177,600

Compare the lender's net of $177,600 sometime in the future to your short-sale offer of $169,000 today. Your offer is now looking very attractive to the lender. The lender will not have to conduct a foreclosure sale. Plus they will not have to wait six to nine months for the property to sell if no one buys the property at the foreclosure sale. Also they will avoid having the holding costs and paying the closing costs. This becomes a win-win deal for you and the lender.

The profit potential for real estate investors to make a profit before, during, or after the foreclosure sale has never been greater. Once there is a negotiated contract with the lender, you as the real estate investor are going to make money. You have bypassed the owner and have dealt directly with the money player—the mortgage lender. This is the essence of the short-sale foreclosure game. Good reading and successful investing!

INTRODUCTION

Over the years we have traveled throughout the country teaching real estate, financial, motivational, and interpersonal skills seminars to our students. We are always striving to be on the leading edge.

Regarding real estate, we have taught everything from buying and selling it creatively as an individual or an investor to core classes for licensing and passing real estate broker's exams. Just about anything you can think of related to real estate, we have taught to someone somewhere!

With a new market come new ideas. We have distilled the knowledge and experience we have gained from buying and selling real estate for ourselves and our clients and helping our students over the last three decades.

Make Money in Short-Sale Foreclosures: How to Bypass Owners and Buy Directly from Lenders is the ninth real estate book we have written. Our first book, *How to Sell Your Home Without a Broker,* is in its fourth edition (2004). Robert J. Bruss, a nationally syndicated real estate columnist, said in his *Los Angeles Times* review of the book: "On a scale of 1 to 10 this book rates a 10" (see book cover).

Our fifth book, *Going Going Gone! Auctioning Your Home for Top Dollar,* was also written to benefit the homeowner in the selling of a home. Like *How to Sell Your Home without a Broker,* our auctioning book was designed to show you how to successfully sell your home and net the most money.

Our sixth book, *The New Path to Real Estate Wealth: Earning Without Owning* (2004), was the first book in our new series designed specifically for active real estate investors. Our Win Going In! series is designed to take you from being a novice real estate investor to being an expert real estate investor.

The New Path to Real Estate Wealth: Earning Without Owning takes you from the real estate basics through the four best ways to make money in real estate. From flipping property to assigning contracts to controlling property using options to buying discount mortgage paper, it teaches you everything you need to know to become a successful real estate investor. In all four areas we train you how to make money without buying or owning property!

Our premise for the Win Going In! series is that no matter what kind of real estate investment you are going to make, you have to win going in. It is no longer enough to make money on the back end of a deal or make a profit when you get out of a deal. The deal has to have a profit built in on the front end, or else you should not do it at all.

Our seventh book, *Quick Cash in Foreclosures* (2004) was the second book in our Win Going In! series. Robert J. Bruss picked this book as one of his top 10 real estate books of 2004. In it we show you how to make money going into a foreclosure deal. It is a hands-on book that teaches you how to enter the real estate foreclosure market and make deals happen. What is unique about the book is that we show you how to have a quick cash investment strategy that you can successfully implement with little or no investment capital.

Our philosophy is that if you can be active in your investment life, you need to be in control of your investments. Counting on a stockbroker, investment adviser, accountant, general partner, or real estate investment fund leaves you completely out of control. When you are an active real estate investor, you are the one calling the shots. You are the one responsible for your successes and failures.

Our eighth book, *Make Money in Real Estate Tax Liens: How to Guarantee Returns Up to 50%* (2005) was the third book in the Win Going In! series. In it we teach you how to make money investing in real estate tax liens. Once a real estate tax lien is placed against real property, one of two things will happen. Either the lien will be paid off by the owner of the property or an investor will buy the lien from the taxing agency that filed it. If the owner of the property does not redeem the lien from the investor, the investor can foreclose on the property and gain an ownership interest.

By investing in real estate tax liens, for pennies on the dollar, you can control a property. Your guarantee is you have the power of foreclosure in the event you are not paid back your original tax lien investment plus hefty interest and penalties. Investing in real estate tax liens is definitely a win going in!

Make Money in Short-Sale Foreclosures: How to Bypass Owners and Buy Directly from Lenders is the fourth book in the Win Going In! series. In this book we teach you how to make money investing in short-sale foreclosures.

A short-sale foreclosure is a mortgage lender accepting less for the loan balance due as a payoff for the loan. Typically, loans are made for no more than 80 percent of the value of the property. In a short-sale you are buying the property for less than the loan amount. This is buying real estate at a wholesale price.

By investing in short-sale foreclosures, you can bypass the owners and buy directly from the lenders. You can do this before, during, or after the foreclosure sale. Whichever way you choose to become involved and invest in short-sale foreclosures, you can make money.

We recommend you read this book in a particular way. Bring a lot of energy to your reading. This does not mean that you have to necessarily read the book quickly, though that is fine with us. We want you to be excited about the material. We want you to win going in as you read.

We suggest that if you find yourself bogging down, stop reading. The material is designed to be comprehended in bursts. See if you can go from one light bulb turning on in your mind to the next. As it gets brighter and brighter, you will find yourself energized.

Our purpose for the Win Going In! series is to teach you all our real estate knowledge and expertise. We want to be the Brain Trust for your successful real estate investments and your lucrative financial investments. The concepts in this book, like all our books, are applicable to most types of real estate just about anywhere. And, like all our books, while we could write using what we refer to as large language, we prefer writing in language understandable by all.

Whether you invest in foreclosures, mortgage notes, or apartment buildings, our goal is for you to get started. You will know you are being a successful investor after you make money on your first real estate deal.

We would love to hear from you about your successes. Also, we want to hear what is working and what is not working for you. Please e-mail us at our new e-mail address, chantalandbillcarey@yahoo.com, or contact us through our publisher, John Wiley & Sons. We are available to help you put your deals together. We are available to partner deals. We also offer various educational and investment programs. Good luck and good deals!

Chantal & Bill Carey

CHAPTER 1

Make Money in Short-Sale Foreclosures

To make money in short-sale foreclosures you must first understand foreclosures. Two strategies to make money in foreclosures are *quick cash* and *long-term wealth building*. Some real estate investors employ the real estate investment strategy of long-term wealth building. In long-term wealth building you buy and hold property for income and appreciation. This can be a very effective strategy in areas of the country that experience very high rates of price appreciation, such as California and the Northeast.

Once you invest your money in real estate, however, it can be difficult to liquidate or sell your assets quickly. Because real estate is the biggest-ticket item for most people, there are the fewest number of buyers in the marketplace compared to most other commodities. The quick cash strategy addresses the problem historically associated with real estate investing: the lack of liquidity.

Quick Cash Strategy

To keep yourself more liquid in your investments, we recommend you use a quick cash strategy to make money in foreclosures. Another name for the quick cash strategy is *flipping*. Flipping is the fastest way to make money in real estate. When you flip a property you get in and out of a property in a short period of time.

Investing in foreclosures can be very cash intensive. When you buy a foreclosure on the courthouse steps, you have to pay cash. Usually there are fix-up expenses with foreclosures that require cash outlays. Also, there may be holding costs like mortgage payments, property taxes, and homeowner's association fees. You may have to flip your foreclosure property so you can get your cash out in order to be able to buy another foreclosure deal.

Top 10 Advantages of the Quick Cash Strategy

The quick cash strategy is especially useful for foreclosure investing. We like quick cash because we do not like landlording (we have tried it), we love the art of the deal (flipping allows you to make lots of deals), and we like making money right away. Here are the top 10 advantages for using the quick cash strategy.

10. No Income Tax Problems

One of the major advantages of the quick cash strategy is you avoid income tax problems. When you hold rental real estate it is very easy to recapture depreciation when you sell the property. Current tax law has you paying a 25 percent tax when you recapture depreciation. How easy is it to recapture depreciation? Just own rental real estate and take depreciation. When you sell the property you will recapture the depreciation.

9. No Extensive Record Keeping

When you own rental real estate you must keep extensive records. You will either have a full-time job as a bookkeeper or you will be paying a bookkeeper. You will have rent receipts, security deposit receipts, and check books (notice we used the plural here). You will have checking accounts to reconcile. How about the legal requirement in some areas of having a trust account for tenant security deposits?

You will keep maintenance records. You may have employees, with all the paperwork and tax nightmares that entails. Items such as worker's compensation insurance, unemployment insurance, health insurance, Occupational Safety and Hazards Association (OSHA), Social Security taxes, and withholding federal income taxes. The list goes on and on.

8. No Lawsuits

If you own real property, there is a very high probability that you will be sued. You will be sued by one of your tenants, their guests, or by a cutthroat attorney. This is the type of attorney who looks up your real estate holdings in the public record to determine whether they will take a case based on the real estate assets you own that they can go after.

When you own property you become a target for frivolous lawsuits. Some of you reading this know exactly what we are talking about because you have been sued for no apparent reason. We also know that some of you have paid legal settlements just to make the frivolous lawsuits go away.

What is our solution? Do not own real property. Not even foreclosure property. The secret is to control real property and not own real property. That is what the quick cash strategy is all about!

7. No Homeowner's Association

If you are, or have ever been, part of a homeowner's association, you know the frustration of dealing with mini tyrants, not to mention the $100, $200, or $300 monthly dues.

Or what about the special assessments for painting, landscaping, or roofing that can run into the thousands of dollars? And, if you do not pay your monthly dues or special assessments, your friendly homeowner's association can foreclose on you and/or sue you.

Homeowner's associations are no longer just attached to condominiums or townhouses. We are seeing an increasing number of maintenance associations attached to planned unit developments (PUDs) and single-family residences (houses).

6. No Repairs and Maintenance Costs

We are sure you have heard the expression *deferred maintenance.* Deferred maintenance is the polite way of saying a property is a fixer-upper. Usually this is because the property owner did not spend any money on regular maintenance through the years. When a property is in foreclosure, you can bet the last thing the property owner will spend money on is repairs and maintenance.

New roof: $7,500. New dishwasher: $400. Gardner: $100 per month. Pool maintenance: $75 per month. Real estate ownership entails significant repairs and maintenance costs. Using a quick cash strategy with property helps you avoid these costs.

5. No Hazard Insurance

No fire insurance, liability insurance, or earthquake insurance. No insurance, period. The last time we checked, any kind of hazard insurance is expensive. And, real estate lenders calculate a monthly insurance payment when qualifying you for a real estate loan, even when you prepay the insurance premium in an escrow account for the next year.

4. No Property Taxes

Depending on your local regulations, you may pay property taxes once a year or perhaps twice a year. In places such as Texas, where there is no state income tax, property taxes can be quite substantial on even modest properties.

For example, on a property valued at $137,000 by the county tax assessor for a particular area in Texas, the annual property tax bill can amount to $4,000! If you calculate that on a monthly basis you are paying $333 a month for every month you own the property.

Monthly Property Taxes

Annual Property Taxes:	$4,000
Monthly Property Taxes:	$333

3. No Monthly Mortgage Payments

Month in and month out, 12 months a year for 30 years. That is 360 payments. Let's look at an example. A $200,000 loan for 30 years at 8 percent interest is payable at $1,467.53 per month, including principal and interest. Multiply the monthly payment by 360 payments and you will pay a total of $528,310.80

Monthly Payments

Monthly Payment	$1,467.53
30 Years	× 360
Total of Payments	$528,310.80

The really nauseating number is when you realize that you originally borrowed $200,000! You wind up paying $328,310.80 in interest. That is 164 percent of the amount you borrowed.

Amount of Interest

Total of Payments	$528,310.80
Amount Borrowed	−$200,000.00
Amount of Interest	$328,310.80

2. No Landlording

There are quite a number of landlording horror stories out there. Do you really think you can be a successful landlord?

Being a landlord is a heartless, thankless job. No matter what you do, you are wrong. Here is a little history with the horror.

Landlording History and Horror Story

Being a lord or a lady of the land has a noble heritage. In olden times there was a symbiotic relationship between the lords and ladies and their tenants. The tenants lived on the lords' and ladies' property, raised their families, and farmed the land.

In return the tenants paid rent to the lords and ladies in the form of most of the crops they grew. There was no money. Or, at least, most people did not have money, like the tenants, because there were no jobs. Everyone's job was working the land.

Unfortunately, this romantic symbiotic relationship from the Middle Ages has been shattered by the realities of today's world. As a landlord you are a target for other people's problems. As a target you become the recipient of a lot of crap. Here are some horrors. (We have so many.) Concrete in the toilet. Concrete in the kitchen sink. Concrete in the oven. Which one would you like to hear? On second thought, we think we will pass. Too many bad memories. Bottom line, we recommend you avoid landlording.

1. Quick Cash

The number one advantage of the quick cash strategy is quick cash. Cash is king! Long live the king! The problem with real estate investing for most people is that it takes far too long to make any money. Yes, we know that if you bought a two bedroom/one bathroom home in Anywhere, California, in 1968 for $20,000, like our friend John did, you would be sitting on a property worth $1 million today. But who has the time or the patience to wait? We do not; do you?

Flipping is your answer. When you are a real estate investor whose strategy is quick cash, patience does not have to be one of your strengths. In fact, being impatient becomes one of your strengths! You become impatient with the deal you are working on and want to get it done so you can get on to the next deal. The more foreclosure deals you get involved with, the more money you will make.

Long-Term Wealth-Building Strategy

We know some of you will prefer using a long-term wealth-building strategy to make money investing in foreclosures. Another way to describe the long-term wealth-building strategy is buying and holding property for income and appreciation.

Top 10 Advantages of Long-Term Wealth Building

We are going to give you the top 10 advantages of using the long-term wealth-building strategy. The long-term wealth-building strategy is also useful for foreclosure investing. Although we prefer the quick cash strategy, you may want to buy and hold your short-sale foreclosure properties. This may be dependent upon in what area of the country you are making your investments.

10. Depreciation

There are income tax advantages for real estate investors who materially participate in the management of their rental properties. You are able to take depreciation on the improvements and use this depreciation to offset the income the property produces.

Let's say you receive $1,300 in monthly rent for 12 months. This is $15,600 in yearly income. If you are able to take $10,000 in annual depreciation, then you will only have to pay taxes on $5,600 in yearly income.

Yearly Income	$15,600
Annual Depreciation	−$10,000
Taxable Income	$5,600

9. Rehabbing

Rehabbing can be an important component in the value of a property. Real estate investors who rehab a foreclosure property contribute not only to their own bottom line but also to the value of the surrounding community.

A property that is rehabbed generates $2 to $3 for every dollar spent rehabbing when you sell the property down the road. If you put $20,000 into rehabbing a property, you can count on a $40,000 to $60,000 value increase as long as you stay within market values for the area in which the property is located.

Rehab Amount	($20,000)
Value Increase	+$60,000
Profit	$40,000

8. Deductibility of Property Taxes

All of the property taxes you pay on the property are tax deductible. When you pay the property taxes, you are able to use this to offset the income the property produces.

Let's say you receive $1,300 in monthly rent for 12 months. This is $15,600 in yearly income. If you pay $5,000 in property taxes, you will have to pay tax on only $10,600 in yearly income.

Yearly Income	$15,600
Property Taxes	−$5,000
Taxable Income	$10,600

7. Deductibility of Mortgage Interest

All of the interest you pay on the mortgages you used to purchase the property is tax deductible. You are able to use the mortgage interest you pay to offset the income the property produces.

Let's say you receive $1,300 in monthly rent for 12 months. This is $15,600 in yearly income. If you pay $8,000 in mortgage interest, then you will only have to pay tax on $7,600 in yearly income.

Yearly Income	$15,600
Mortgage Interest	−$8,000
Taxable Income	$7,600

If we put depreciation, property tax, and mortgage interest deductibility together from our examples, we would have $10,000, $5,000, and $8,000 respectively. This totals $23,000.

Annual Depreciation	$10,000
Property Taxes	$5,000
Mortgage Interest	+$8,000
Total Deduction	$23,000

This easily offsets our $15,600 in rental income. In fact, the $7,400 excess deduction may be used to offset other income. Check with your tax adviser.

Yearly Income	$15,600
Total Deduction	($23,000)
Excess Deduction	($7,400)

6. Long-Term Capital Gains

You receive long-term capital gains tax treatment for property held longer than one year. This can be a huge tax savings compared to being taxed at ordinary income tax rates. Comparing an ordinary income tax rate of 28 percent with a long-term capital gains rate of 15 percent, you can see that you practically cut your tax bill in half.

Let's say you have a profit of $50,000. At a 28 percent ordinary income tax rate you would pay $14,000 in income tax. At a 15 percent long-term capital gains rate you would pay $7,500 in income tax. You save $6,500 in taxes.

Ordinary Income Tax Rate (28%)	$14,000
Capital Gains Tax Rate (15%)	−$7,500
Tax Savings	$6,500

5. 1031 Tax Deferred Exchanges

You can defer income tax consequences by doing a 1031 tax deferred exchange. Even with favorable long-term capital gains treatment, your tax bill can still be quite substantial.

Let's say you have a long-term capital gain of $200,000. At a 15 percent long-term capital gain tax rate, your tax bill will be $30,000 if you sell the property.

Long-Term Capital Gain	$200,000
Long-Term Capital Gains Tax Rate	×15%
Taxes You Owe	$30,000

By doing a 1031 tax deferred exchange you will defer having the $200,000 long-term gain recognized. Because the gain is not recognized, there is no tax consequence to you at the time of the sale. You have an additional $30,000 in your pocket to make another real estate investment.

4. Economies of Scale

A nice advantage of long-term wealth building is being able to use the economies of scale as a landlord. When you have accumulated 5, 10, or 15 properties, you can begin a cookie-cutter property management style.

If there is a sale on paint, you buy paint for all your properties. If there is a sale on carpeting or flooring, you buy carpeting or flooring for all your properties. By buying in bulk you save money. It is like buying wholesale instead of retail.

3. Cash Flow

People who use the long-term wealth-building strategy want to build in cash flow for any properties they are going to keep. Cash flow contributes to your overall bottom line.

When your income exceeds your expenses, you have positive cash flow. This is a good thing. When your expenses exceed your income, you have negative cash flow, which is, of course, a bad thing.

2. Appreciation

When the market is hot, the market is hot! Like our example of the two bedroom/one bathroom home in Anywhere, California, that our friend John bought in 1968 for $20,000 that is now worth $1 million. Every real estate market appreciates. Some markets appreciate at a much higher rate than others. Take a look at the net differences between these various market appreciation rates.

If you are in a market that appreciates at 4 percent annually, property values will double every 18 years. If you are in a market that appreciates at 7 percent annually, property values will double every 10 years. If you are in a market that appreciates at 12 percent annually, property values will double every six years. Consider what your investment goals are when choosing the market area for your long-term wealth building.

1. Long-Term Wealth Building

The number one advantage of the long-term wealth-building strategy is long-term wealth building. You are building a future nest egg by using this strategy. By holding property, you are compounding your equity year after year without any income tax consequence.

Although the quick cash strategy brings you quick cash, unless you are disciplined enough to save or reinvest some of your quick cash, it will disappear as quickly as it came. The future is going to come no matter which investment strategy you choose. You have to decide if long-term wealth building or quick cash will work best for accomplishing your real estate foreclosure investment goals.

We are now going to get into the foreclosure arena. Starting from the basics, we will show you how to apply the quick cash or long-term wealth-building strategy to your foreclosure investing. For those of you who are knowledgeable about foreclosures, we recommend you go to Chapter 3, "What Is a Short-Sale Foreclosure?" For those of you who are new to the foreclosure game, we recommend you read straight through the book, continuing with Chapter 2, "What Is a Foreclosure?"

What Is a Foreclosure?

The economy and the real estate market are cyclical. Over the next three years as interest rates rise and the housing market cools, there are going to be many foreclosure opportunities. There is a lot of money to be made in the real estate foreclosure market. You have to be very knowledgeable about traditional foreclosures before you get involved with short-sale foreclosures.

We are going to spend some time training you in the foreclosure process. Every area has a slightly different method on how it handles foreclosure procedures; however, the basic process is the same most everywhere.

What varies from one area to another is the time periods allowed for foreclosure. Do not get too caught up in what may seem to be very technical information. We present this information so you can get the sense of what is involved in a foreclosure. Use this chapter as your foreclosure reference guide.

Foreclosure

There is no more dreaded word in the real estate world than *foreclosure*. It does not matter if you are the real estate borrower or the real estate lender. No one likes to be in a foreclosure situation.

Foreclosure is when a real estate lender, whether an institutional real estate lender or a private real estate lender, takes the title to a property away from the borrower in lieu of receiving mortgage payments. Said more formally, when all else has failed, a real estate lender will pursue allowed legal prerogatives to recover the collateral for the real estate loan in order to sell it and recoup their loan proceeds.

The definition of foreclosure is to shut out, exclude, bar, or deprive a person of the right to redeem a mortgage. Foreclosure is not only a process to recover a lender's collateral but also a procedure whereby a borrower's rights of redemption are eliminated and all interests in the subject property are removed. Let's start with the power of sale foreclosure.

Power of Sale Foreclosure

A power of sale foreclosure is based on the terms of the deed of trust or the mortgage contract, giving the lender, or the trustee, the right to sell the collateral property without being required to spend the time and money involved in a court foreclosure suit. Let's use Texas to illustrate an example of a power of sale foreclosure.

In Texas these nonjudicial foreclosures are more common than judicial foreclosures (lawsuits in court). The right to exercise the power of sale must be created in writing and is usually part of the deed of trust, which must clearly state that there is a right of nonjudicial foreclosure. The power of sale foreclosure is popular in Texas because it allows the trustee to sell the property more quickly and thus recover the lender's collateral in a timely manner.

The trustee named in the deed of trust has the power to sell the defaulted mortgaged property upon the request of the real estate lender or beneficiary of the trust deed. The trustee must then carefully follow the terms and conditions stated in the deed of trust for the foreclosure. The foreclosure sale must also follow the legal procedures of the state of Texas.

Texas Property Code

The Texas Property Code contains the following procedures for nonjudicial foreclosure. You can check what your area procedures are by contacting a real estate attorney or your local title insurance company.

1. The trustee must notify the debtor of the foreclosure sale at least 21 days before the date of the sale. This notice is to be sent by certified mail to the debtor's last known address.
2. Notice must be posted at the courthouse door of the county in which the property is located and filed in the county clerk's office where the sale is to be held.
3. The sale must be a public auction held between 10:00 A.M. and 4:00 P.M. on the first Tuesday of the month.
4. The sale must take place in the county where the property is located.
5. The holder of the debt on residential property must give the debtor at least 20 days to cure the default before the entire debt can be accelerated and declared due and the notice of sale given.

At the Foreclosure Sale

At the foreclosure sale, the trustee has an obligation to act impartially and can take no action that would discourage bidders. This is to be a public auction open to all persons, including the lender and the trustee.

There is no requirement in Texas that the auction generate fair market value; therefore, the property will go to the highest cash bidder. The purchaser of the foreclosed property takes the title without any covenants through an instrument called a trustee's deed.

The proceeds from the sale will be used to pay the trustee and any expenses of the trustee's sale. Then the lender who is foreclosing will be paid. If there is any money left, those creditors who had filed liens against the property will be paid. Finally, any surplus monies must be returned to the borrower/debtor.

In Texas, as in every other state in the United States, if a senior lien holder forecloses, all junior lien holders' interests terminate. If a junior lien holder forecloses, they get the title to the property subject to the senior lien holders' interests in the property. Our international readers can check what local customary actions to take for terminating liens. Now let's talk about judicial foreclosure and sale.

Judicial Foreclosure and Sale

Judicial foreclosure and sale is a legal procedure that involves the use of the courts and the consequent sale of the collateral. Foreclosure by court order is an alternative method that may be used in Texas, and other places, although it is not favored by commercial lenders. It is the only remedy if a deed of trust does not contain a power of sale provision.

How a Judicial Foreclosure and Sale Works

The delinquent mortgagors are notified of the default and the reasons for it. They are also informed that an immediate solution is required and that all their efforts must be expended to solve the problem as quickly as possible.

If all attempts fail, however, a complaint is filed by the lender in the court for the county in which the property is located and a summons is issued to the borrowers. This initiates the foreclosure process.

Simultaneously, a title search is made to determine the identities of all parties having an interest in the collateral property, and a *lis pendens* (literally, a legal action pending) is filed with the court, giving notice to the world of the pending foreclosure action.

Notice is sent to all parties having an interest in the property, requesting that they appear in court in order to defend their interests, or else they will be foreclosed (shut out, excluded, barred, or deprived) from any future rights by judgment of the court. It is vitally important for the complainant lender to notify all junior lien holders of the foreclosure action so they will not be enjoined (prohibited) from participation in the property auction. If junior lien holders are not given proper notice, they acquire the right to file suit on their own at some future time.

Jurisdiction

Depending upon the number of days required by the presiding jurisdiction for public notice to be given to inform any and all persons having an unrecorded interest in the subject property that a foreclosure suit is imminent, and depending upon the availability of a court date, the complaint is eventually aired before a presiding judge. In most instances, the defendant borrower does not appear in court unless special circumstances are presented in defense of the default.

Those creditors who do appear to present their claims are recognized and noted, and a sale of the property at a public auction by a court-appointed referee or the sheriff is ordered by means of a judgment decree. The proceeds from the sale will be used to satisfy the parties named in the judgment. The borrower's right to redeem the property continues for a reasonable time after the sale.

In a judicial foreclosure a junior lien holder's interest in the property is not automatically eliminated. If the junior lien holder did not join in the foreclosure suit, the property is sold subject to the junior lien. If, however, the junior lien holder was a party to the foreclosure suit, this interest ends at the sale in the same way as the senior lien holder's interest does. Now we are going to look at insured mortgage foreclosures.

Insured Conventional Mortgage Foreclosure

Under the terms of the insurance policies of most private mortgage guarantee companies (private mortgage insurance, or PMI), a default is interpreted to be nonpayment for four months. Within 10 days of default, the lender is required to notify the private mortgage insurer, who will then decide whether to instruct the lender to foreclose.

When an insured conventional mortgage is foreclosed, the lender who is insured is the original bidder at the public auction of the collateral property. Under these circumstances, the successful bidder lender files notice with the insurance company within 60 days after the legal proceedings have transpired.

Loss Recovery

If the insurance company is confident of recovering any losses by purchasing the collateral property from the lender and then reselling it, it will reimburse the lender for the total amount of the lender's bid and receive title to the property.

If, however, the private mortgage insurance company does not foresee any possibility for recovery, it may elect to pay the lender the agreed-upon amount of insurance, and the lender retains ownership of the property. The lender then sells the property to recover any balance still unpaid.

Private mortgage insurance will play a role in a lender agreeing to do a short-sale. If private mortgage insurance agrees to compensate the lender for part of the lender's loss, the lender may be willing to do a short-sale with you at a greatly reduced loan payoff. We will give you all the details in Chapter 13, "FHA, VA, and Private Mortgage Insurance Short-Sales."

Remember that, in any and all cases of judicial foreclosure and sale, any ownership rights acquired by the successful bidder at the foreclosure auction will still be subject to the statutory redemption rights of the defaulted mortgagor. A full fee simple absolute title cannot vest in the winning bidder until these redemption rights have expired.

A property title vests, or becomes valid, when you receive full ownership rights in a property. Another way to say this is that once there is a vesting of title, your interest in the property cannot be voided.

Federal Housing Administration Insured Mortgage Foreclosure

Foreclosures on Federal Housing Administration (FHA) insured mortgages originate with the filing of form 2068 Notice of Default by the lender. This form must be given to the local FHA administrative office within 60 days of default. The notice describes the reasons for the mortgagor's delinquency, such as death, illness, marital difficulties, income loss, excessive financial obligations, employment transfers, or military service.

In many cases involving delinquent FHA insured mortgages, loan counselors from the local FHA office will attempt to design an agreement between the lender and the borrower for adjustments to the loan conditions in order to prevent foreclosure. The most common technique used in circumstances in which default is beyond the borrower's control, but deemed curable, is known as forbearance of foreclosure.

Forbearance of foreclosure is when a lender does not proceed to formally filing a foreclosure action even though the lender has the legal right to do so. An agreement is signed by the lender and the borrower to handle the back payments. This allows the borrower to remain in the property.

Default Not Cured

If the problems causing the default are solved within a one-year period, the lender informs the local FHA office of that fact. If not, a default status report is filed, and the lender must initiate foreclosure proceedings. If the bids at the foreclosure auction are less than the unpaid mortgage balance, the lender is expected to bid the debt, take title to the property, and present it to the FHA along with a claim for insurance, which may be paid in cash or in government securities. In some cases, with prior FHA approval, the lender may assign the defaulted mortgage directly to the FHA before the final foreclosure action in exchange for insurance benefits.

In any case, if the property can be sold easily at a price that would repay the loan in full, the lender simply would sell the property after winning the bid at the foreclosure auction and would not apply for FHA compensation. If the property cannot be sold at a price that would repay the loan in full, however, then the lender will involve the FHA.

Like most lenders, the FHA would prefer not to be in the property owning business. If the FHA ends up as the owner of the property, the property may be sold as is. However, the FHA may repair or refurbish (fix up) the property if it feels the property can be resold at a higher price and minimize the losses to the FHA.

The FHA will consider and participate in a short-sale if it saves the FHA money. Again, we will give you information on FHA short-sales in Chapter 13.

Veterans Affairs Guaranteed Mortgage Foreclosure

Unlike the FHA insured mortgage, whereby a lender's entire risk is recovered from the insurance benefits, a Department of Veterans Affairs (VA) loan is similar to a privately insured loan in that a lender receives only the top portion of the outstanding loan balance, up to a statutory limit.

Let's say the veteran borrowed $100,000 from a VA approved lender. The VA will guarantee the top $25,000. The lender will be responsible for the remaining $75,000. If the loss exceeds the VA guaranteed $25,000, the lender will be responsible for any excess above the $25,000.

Amount Borrowed	$100,000
VA Guaranteed	−$25,000
Lender Responsibility	$75,000

In the event a delinquency of more than three months of payments on a VA loan, the lender must file proper notification with the local VA office, which may then elect to bring the loan current if it wishes. If this occurs, the VA can come against the defaulting veteran for repayment of the funds advanced.

Like the FHA

Much like the FHA, VA lenders are required to make every effort to help the borrower through forbearance, payment adjustments, a deed in lieu of foreclosure (more about this shortly), or other acceptable solution. Actual foreclosure is only considered as a last resort.

In the event of a foreclosure, the lender usually will be the original bidder at the auction and will submit a claim for losses to the local VA office. The Department of Veterans Affairs has the option to pay the unpaid balance, interest, and any court costs and then take title to the property.

The VA can require that the lender keep the property. They may do this if the property has badly deteriorated. This would reinforce the importance for the lender to supervise the condition of the property. The VA would pay the lender the difference between the determined value of the property on the date of the foreclosure sale and the remaining mortgage balance. We will talk about VA short-sales in Chapter 13. Let's move on to second mortgage foreclosures.

Second Mortgage Foreclosure

Defaults of second mortgages and other junior mortgages are handled exactly in the same manner as conventional first mortgages. Here, however, the relationship is usually, but not always, between two individuals rather than between an institutional lender and an individual borrower.

A second mortgagee will usually seek the counsel of an attorney to manage the foreclosure process against a second mortgagor. The delinquent borrower will be requested to cure the problem within a certain time period. If a cure cannot be accomplished, notice is given to all persons having an interest in the property, and the attorney then files for judicial foreclosure.

The second mortgagee generally is the original bidder at the public sale and secures ownership of the collateral property subject to the lien of the existing first mortgage. They can then continue to maintain the integrity of this first mortgage by making any payments required while seeking to sell the collateral to eliminate, or at least offset, any losses.

Deficiency Judgments

If the proceeds from a foreclosure sale are not sufficient to recover the outstanding loan balance plus the costs incurred as a consequence of default and interest to date, a lender may, in most places, sue on the mortgage for the deficiency.

If the foreclosure is by court order, the judge normally awards the lender a judgment against the debtor in the amount of the deficiency. If a power of sale foreclosure took place, the lender must then file suit against the debtor to collect any deficiency.

For example, in Texas, a lender would consider several things before pursuing legal action for a deficiency balance because the amount of the deficiency and the ability of the debtor to pay after the suit would be important factors.

The homestead laws in Texas, as in many other places, protect most of the debtor's basic possessions from this type of judgment. In most cases, a defaulted borrower does not have any nonexempt assets to make up this deficiency. Otherwise, they would have been put to use in order to prevent the default in the first place.

Current Trend

The current trend is to rely less on collecting deficiencies and more on limiting a borrower's personal liability on a real estate loan to the equity in the collateral property. Especially on purchase-money loans, lenders may be limited to recovering only the collateral property and nothing more.

This is a positive development for short-sale investing. Most borrowers initially borrow money to purchase real estate. These borrowers get into financial trouble in the initial two or three years. They typically have little or no equity built up in the property. All the lender can do is foreclose on the property.

If the sale of the property does not fully compensate the lender for what they are owed, that is too bad for the lender. The lender cannot go after the borrower personally for any deficiencies. (The one caveat to this is that the VA can and will go after the defaulting veteran.) It may be in the lender's best interest to dispose of the property via a short-sale deal with investors.

Lender Adjustments

A lender will usually attempt to adjust the conditions of a loan in order to help a troubled borrower over short-term difficulties. Delinquent mortgage payments are the most common cause for a default. The nonpayment of property taxes or hazard insurance premiums, lack of adequate maintenance, and allowing priority liens to take effect are also cause for default.

To offset the possibility of a foreclosure on delinquent mortgages, many lenders will exercise forbearance and waive the principal portion of a loan payment for a while or even extend a moratorium on the full monthly payment until a borrower can better arrange their finances. Other adjustments in terms of a delinquent mortgage that might aid the defaulted borrower include an extension of time or a recasting of the loan to reflect the borrower's current ability to pay under circumstances of financial distress.

Take a Deed in Lieu of Foreclosure

A lender may encourage a hopelessly defaulted borrower to voluntarily give a deed to the property to the lender. This is called a deed in lieu of foreclosure. By executing either a quitclaim deed or a grant deed, a borrower can eliminate the stigma of a foreclosure, maintain a respectable credit rating, and avoid the possibility of a deficiency judgment.

The lender must take care to be protected against any future claims of fraud or duress by the borrower, however. In addition, the lender must be aware of the possibility of the existence of other liens, like IRS liens, filed against the property.

Sell the Mortgage

Sometimes all efforts to adjust the terms of a mortgage to solve a borrower's problems fail. A lender may then attempt to sell the loan. This creates another opportunity for you as a real estate investor. We will explore this possibility in Chapter 14, "Buying the Mortgage in Foreclosure at a Short-Sale Price."

Do a Short-Sale

Real estate lenders are fully aware of the difficulties with and the costs and time involved in a full foreclosure process. If the lender cannot find a buyer willing and able to buy the loan, the lender may be open to an investor willing to do a short-sale. The short-sale allows the lender to avoid the costly and time-consuming process of foreclosure.

Wrap-up

This chapter provided an overview of the foreclosure process. By far the greatest number of real estate financing arrangements do not result in problems leading to foreclosure.

Historically rising property values coupled with the systematic repayment of loans created measurable equity positions for borrowers. A troubled borrower could, in most problem situations, arrange to dispose of his or her property and thus maintain financial equilibrium.

This is what gave you, as a real estate investor, an opportunity to help someone in financial distress and still make a profit. When misfortune could not be averted and foreclosure developed as the sole remedy, this provided the motivation to the borrower with equity to be open to your help.

Recently, because of overly aggressive lending practices, including interest-only or negatively amortized loans, and the cooling of some real estate markets, there are borrowers who are getting into a financial bind that do not have a measurable equity position in their property. This is creating an unprecedented short-sale investment opportunity.

In Chapter 3 we will explain short-sale foreclosures. Equipped with the knowledge and information in this book, you will be positioned to take complete advantage of this historic short-sale opportunity. A short-sale foreclosure is a lender agreeing to a sale of a property for less than the loan amount. You are able to buy property at a wholesale price.

CHAPTER **3**

What Is a Short-Sale Foreclosure?

A short-sale foreclosure is a lender selling a property for less than the loan amount. Foreclosures come in all shapes and sizes. Any property that has a real estate loan attached to it is a short-sale foreclosure waiting to happen. Borrowers get behind in their mortgage payments for all sorts of reasons. What is worse, people can lose their property to a foreclosure without having any real estate loans attached to the property.

If you do not pay your local property taxes, your local taxing authority can place a lien against your property. If you do not pay the property taxes within a certain period of time after the lien is filed, then the local taxing authority sells your property at a foreclosure sale for the back taxes. (See our book *Make Money in Real Estate Tax Liens: How to Guarantee Returns Up to 50%,* John Wiley & Sons, 2005.)

You can own your property free and clear (no real estate loans) and be sued. If you lose the lawsuit, your property can be taken to satisfy the judgment. If you cannot pay the judgment, your property will be sold at a sheriff's sale to the highest bidder.

You can be current on your monthly real estate loan payments or own your property free and clear and you can be current on your local property taxes. You are not even being sued. You are in trouble with the Internal Revenue Service, however. The IRS places a tax lien against your property. Eventually, if you do not work something out with the IRS, they will seize your property and sell it at a foreclosure sale.

All of these foreclosure events create foreclosure opportunities for you as a real estate investor. From a quick cash strategy point of view, foreclosures give you the possibility to flip either the property or the real estate contract associated with the property. From a long-term wealth-building point of view, foreclosures give you the possibility to buy real estate wholesale and hold it for income and appreciation.

Four Reasons to Buy Foreclosures

We are going to give you four reasons to buy foreclosures. One of these reasons by itself is enough to make foreclosures a good investment. Short-sale foreclosures are a specialized type of foreclosure. Therefore, investing in short-sale foreclosures is a specialized type of foreclosure investing.

When you buy foreclosures you are buying wholesale real estate, you are buying from a wholesale seller, you have less competition than buying retail property, and you have the opportunity to make quick cash or acquire a good property for your real estate portfolio.

1. Buying Wholesale Real Estate

Foreclosures are by definition wholesale real estate. Why would you want to pay retail for anything that you can buy wholesale? Real estate is the same way. When you are buying foreclosures you are buying real estate at a wholesale price. Because real estate is usually the highest priced commodity that people buy, when you buy real estate wholesale, you have an opportunity to make a lot of money.

You might think that foreclosure properties are run-down or in poor shape. Although this is certainly the case for some of the foreclosure properties that we have been involved with, it is not always the case. You might also think foreclosure properties are in bad neighborhoods. Again, although that can be the case, we have found foreclosures in some very nice neighborhoods that were in very good condition.

Real Estate Lenders

Ninety-five percent of the foreclosure market begins and ends with real estate lenders. When you understand how lenders operate, you will increase the likelihood of being successful with foreclosure investing. This is especially true for short-sale foreclosure investing.

There are two keys to understanding how lenders operate: (1) lenders get the money they make real estate loans with at a wholesale interest rate and (2) lenders only make wholesale real estate loans at usually no more than an 80 percent loan to the value of the property.

Let's look at how real estate lenders operate in the real estate market. Real estate lenders make money by loaning money. How lenders get the money to loan is from people like you and us. When people put money in the bank, the bank pays them interest for their money. When the bank loans money to someone to buy real estate, it loans the money for the real estate loan at a higher interest rate than the bank pays in interest to its customers.

Wholesale Interest

You could say that the bank pays a wholesale interest rate to get its money and then receives a retail interest rate when it loans its money. For example, a bank may pay 3 percent interest to its customers for certificates of deposit (CDs). Then the bank turns around and loans the money from the CDs to real estate borrowers for real estate loans at 7 percent interest.

That is a spread of 4 percentage points. The bank makes money on the spread between the wholesale interest rate it pays on the CDs and the retail interest rate it charges on the real estate loans.

Rule of 72

This is a good place to teach you the Rule of 72. The Rule of 72 states that whatever annual rate of return you receive on your investment, real estate or otherwise, your investment will double in the number of years you get as the answer to dividing the rate of return into 72.

The Rule of 72 assumes you leave the investment return with the investment each year so you are compounding your investment return. We will assume your investment is in a tax-free or tax-deferred vehicle.

Real estate appreciation works well with the Rule of 72. If your property appreciated 6 percent annually, it would double in value in 12 years (6 goes into 72 12 times).

Back to the real estate lender. If you receive 3 percent annual interest on $200,000 worth of CDs, then according to the Rule of 72 your $200,000 will become $400,000 in 24 years (3 goes into 72 24 times). If the real estate lender receives 7 percent annual interest on $200,000 worth of real estate loans, then according to the Rule of 72 their $200,000 will become $400,000 in 10 years (7 goes into 72 10 times).

Certificates of Deposit	Real Estate Loans
$200,000 @ 3%	$200,000 @ 7%
$72 \div 3 = 24$ Years	$72 \div 7 = 10$ Years
Doubles to	Doubles to
$400,000	$400,000

What is truly amazing about these numbers is if we look at them over the course of a 30-year real estate loan. Your $200,000 in CDs will double once to $400,000 in 24 years. Over the next six years (from 24 years to 30 years), your $400,000 will become $500,000.

What do you think will happen to the bank's $200,000? The bank's $200,000 will double to $400,000 after 10 years, as we have already noted. The $400,000 will double to $800,000 in another 10 years (20 years total). The $800,000 will double to $1.6 million in another 10 years (30 years total). The lender will have to give $500,000 to you for your $200,000 in CDs plus interest. The lender will make $1.1 million profit!

Certificates of Deposit	Real Estate Loans
$200,000 @ 3%	$200,000 @ 7%
in 30 Years	in 30 Years

Becomes	Becomes
$500,000	$1,600,000

Now you know why real estate lenders want to be in the real estate lending business. They make so much money on the interest rate spread. Real estate lenders do not want to be in the real estate owning business. This is a key factor in why real estate lenders will agree to make short-sale foreclosure deals.

Wholesale Loans

Real estate lenders will loan only 80 percent of the appraised value of the real estate to protect themselves in the event the borrower defaults on their loan payments. In other words, a real estate lender will make only a wholesale real estate loan. The amount the lender loans is called the loan to value ratio. How much money would a bank loan on a property that was appraised (valued) for $200,000?

Loan to Value Ratio

Appraised Value	$200,000
Maximum Loan Percentage	×80%
Maximum Loan Amount	$160,000

As you can see from the previous numbers, real estate lenders protect themselves by making sure they have a 20 percent cushion between the appraised value, $200,000, and the loan value, $160,000. This $40,000 cushion is typically the borrower's down payment on the property. Even if the borrower defaults to the tune of $10,000, the lender is protected.

Lender Protection

Appraised Value	$200,000
Maximum Loan Amount	−$160,000
Default Amount	−$10,000
Lender Protection	$30,000
Lender Loss	0

What about real estate lenders who loan 90 percent or 95 percent of the retail value? Won't that put them in jeopardy in the event of a default?

That is where private mortgage insurance (PMI) companies step in. For an insurance premium paid by the borrower, the private mortgage insurer will insure the real estate lender for any defaults above an 80 percent loan to value ratio.

Let's say the borrower received a 90 percent loan from the lender ($180,000) and made only a 10 percent down payment ($20,000) on the same $200,000 property.

Loan to Value Ratio

Appraised Value	$200,000
Loan Percentage	×90%
Loan Amount	$180,000

With the same $10,000 borrower default, the lender still has $10,000 of cushion for the loan they made.

Lender Protection

Appraised Value	$200,000
Maximum Loan Amount	−$180,000
Default Amount	−$10,000
Lender Protection	$10,000
Lender Loss	0

Even if the borrower defaulted in the amount of $25,000, the private mortgage insurance would pick up the additional $5,000 beyond the borrower's $20,000 equity (down payment). This is another reason why real estate lenders will agree to make short-sale foreclosure deals. The amount of money they may be out beyond the loan amount may be covered by private mortgage insurance.

Private Mortgage Insurance

Appraised Value	$200,000
Maximum Loan Amount	−$180,000
Default Amount	−$25,000
Lender Protection	($5,000)

Private Mortgage Insurance $5,000
Lender Loss   0

2. Buying from a Wholesale Seller

It is important to identify who sells wholesale or foreclosure property. Once you know who the sellers are, you can prepare your strategy to achieve the best results. There are only three sellers of foreclosure property.

Two of the sellers have a big financial stake in the property. One of the sellers has no financial stake in the property. Two of the sellers are professional sellers. One of the sellers is not.

Buying from the Seller in Distress

The seller in distress has a big financial stake in the property. Not only will it destroy their credit if their property goes to a foreclosure sale, but they will lose all their equity in the property. Obviously, the seller in distress is not a professional seller.

We will use some of the numbers we have already shown to illustrate our point. The appraised value of the property is $200,000. The loan amount on the property is $160,000. The borrower is in default in the amount of $10,000. The borrower's equity position before the default is $40,000.

Where does the borrower's $10,000 default amount get deducted from? As we have already seen, the $10,000 default amount comes out of the borrower's $40,000 equity. The farther the borrower gets behind in their mortgage payments, the more of the borrower's remaining equity is eaten up.

Your mission with sellers in distress is to show them how to avoid the foreclosure sale. You are going to become an educator to the seller in distress. You will make an appointment with them and, at the appointment, will educate them on their eight foreclosure options.

Hopefully, for their sake, you will be able to get the information to them before it is too late. One of the foreclosure options you will present is for them to sell you their equity. You can only pay them a wholesale price. They will get some of their equity back if they work with you. If the property goes to the foreclosure sale, they will get none of their equity back.

You might offer them $9,000 for their remaining $30,000 equity. Remember, you will still have to come up with an additional $10,000 to make up the default to the lender. You would now have $19,000 in the property ($9,000 to the seller and $10,000 to the lender).

You would also get the property subject to the $160,000 loan. Your total in the property would be $179,000. The property is worth $200,000. You have a $21,000 profit potential, which is more than a 100 percent return on your $19,000 investment.

Profit Potential

Loan Amount	$160,000
Buy Seller's Equity	$9,000
Default Amount	+$10,000
Amount in Property	$179,000
Appraised Value	$200,000
Amount in Property	−$179,000
Profit Potential	$21,000
Profit Potential	$21,000
Cash Invested	$19,000
Investment Return	111%

Buying at the Foreclosure Sale

Foreclosure sales are conducted at a public auction. The highest bidder gets the property. The seller at the foreclosure sale is a trustee or representative of the lender, so the seller at the foreclosure sale is really like an auctioneer. They are professional sellers, yet they do not have any financial stake in the property. They are just doing their job.

Once it gets to the foreclosure sale, the owners are out of luck. If you have not been able to help them or work out a purchase for their equity, the owner will lose all of their equity at the foreclosure sale.

You must have cash or cashier's checks to bid at the foreclosure sale. It is best to check with the foreclosure sale seller before the actual foreclosure sale date to find out how the seller wants payment.

Credit Bid

The opening bid is called a *credit bid.* The credit bid is put forward by the trustee or the representative of the lender. The credit bid is the total of the remaining loan balance, payments in default, and any costs associated with the foreclosure sale. If no one bids above the credit bid, then the lender winds up owning the property. Any bid made above the credit bid must be made in cash. Let's say the foreclosure sale expenses are $1,900. What would the opening credit bid be? Again we will continue to use the same numbers we have used throughout this chapter.

Opening Credit Bid

Loan Amount	$160,000
Default Amount	$10,000
Foreclosure Expenses	$1,900
Credit Bid	$171,900

Winning the Bid

What if you bid one dollar more than the opening credit bid? If you could buy the property at the foreclosure sale for $171,901 would that be a better deal than if you could have bought the property from the owner before the foreclosure sale for $179,000?

The answer is that it depends. Although it certainly looks like getting the property at the foreclosure sale for $7,099 less is the better deal, maybe it is not the better deal. This is a price versus terms conversation.

You get a better price at the foreclosure sale. But you have to come up with almost $172,000! Buying from the seller you did not get as good a price: $179,000. But you only have $19,000 in the deal. Will that $7,000 lower price be worth tying up an additional $153,000?

Buying from the Lender

What about buying from the lender after the foreclosure sale? Usually, the lender has the biggest financial stake in the property. After all, they originally made an 80 percent loan to the borrower to buy the property. Can you get a better deal from the lender once the property goes out of the lender's loan portfolio and into the lender's property portfolio?

Lenders' property portfolios are called real estate owned portfolios, or REOs. Real estate lenders are in the business of making real estate loans. Real estate lender's are not in the business of owning real estate.

Although lenders want to sell their REOs for as much as possible, they want to move these REO properties as quickly as possible. After all, we know what they are going to do with the money they get from selling the property. They are going to make another real estate loan!

Depending on the real estate lender, you may be able to pick up this REO property from them in the neighborhood of $155,000 to $165,000. Sounds like the best deal in the price department. What about the terms department? Ah, there is the rub. Are you going to have to put up a lot of cash and qualify for a new loan?

Although real estate lenders are professional sellers, sometimes their own bureaucracy gets in the way of them making an effective deal. Our recommendation to you is to work with several lenders' REO departments and see what happens.

Of course, if you can arrange a short-sale with the lender before the foreclosure sale, this may be an even better option. You may find the lender's loss mitigation side more profitable to deal with than the lender's REO side.

3. Less Competition than Retail

As competitive as the foreclosure market may seem, there are fewer buyers in the foreclosure market than in the retail market. The short-sale foreclosure market has even less competition. Of the total number of real estate mortgages, typically 2 percent of them will be in the foreclosure process at any one time. Once you become familiar with the material in this book, you will know more than 98 percent of the people trying to make money investing in foreclosures.

You will know more about foreclosures than 99 percent of the attorneys out there unless they specialize in foreclosures.

The point is that we think one of the best reasons to check out the foreclosure scene is there really is very little knowledgeable competition. There is even less knowledgeable competition in the short-sale foreclosure scene.

4. Make Quick Cash or Build Long-Term Wealth

You can make quick cash or build long-term wealth in the foreclosure arena. You can work with the seller in distress before the foreclosure process gets too far down the line. We call this the preforeclosure stage. Once you make a deal with the seller in distress, you can either flip your foreclosure real estate contract for quick cash or keep the property for yourself to build long-term wealth.

Assign Foreclosure Contracts for Quick Cash

You may find it easier to assign foreclosure contracts than it is to assign nonforeclosure contracts. When people in general, and real estate investors in particular, hear the word *foreclosure,* they automatically think there might be a good deal available. When you drop the word *foreclosure* at a social gathering, everyone turns around to catch the conversation.

Build Long-Term Wealth

We present the following information for those of you who would like to build long-term wealth from your foreclosure investing. In the 1990s in California there was a company called Rent Busters. It offered foreclosed homes to buyers for no down payment. The concept was simple. The company would advertise for people to find foreclosure deals.

The company was paid $1,500 by a client to take the client to a foreclosure sale to buy the client a property. The client had to agree to go to 10 foreclosure sales. If, after going to 10 foreclosure sales, Rent Busters had not bought the client a property, the client got the $1,500 back.

If Rent Busters did buy a property at one of the 10 foreclosure sales, the client's $1,500 would be applied to closing costs. The company would go to the foreclosure sale and buy the property. It would pay no more than 80 percent of the retail value. Of course, because the company was buying the property at the foreclosure sale, it would pay cash.

Then Rent Busters would sell the property to the people who had brought the foreclosure to them. They would sell the property to the client for no money down. Rent Busters would carry the down payment back in a promissory note secured by a second mortgage.

The client would get a new 80 percent loan on the property. The proceeds of the loan would go to Rent Busters as the seller. This would replenish the cash that Rent Busters used to purchase the property at the foreclosure sale. Then the down payment financing would become the profit for Rent Busters collected over the agreed time frame.

Example

Let's say Rent Busters got a $200,000 property for $160,000 at the foreclosure sale and financed the $40,000 down payment for the buyer for three years at 10 percent annual interest.

Foreclosure Sale

Retail Value	$200,000
Foreclosure Price	−$160,000
Equity for Rent Busters	$40,000

Sale to Client

Purchase Price	$200,000
New Financing	−$160,000
Seller Financing	$40,000

Profit to Rent Busters

Seller Financing	$40,000
10% for 3 Years	+$12,000
Gross Profit	$52,000

Summary

When you buy foreclosures you are buying wholesale real estate, you are buying from a wholesale seller, you have less competition than buying retail property, and you have the opportunity to make quick cash or build long-term wealth.

In the next chapter we will teach you how to find short-sale foreclosures. The key for us is to get to the seller in distress before another investor does. Once you have located a seller in distress, you get their permission to talk to the real estate lender. This is your entry point to bypassing the owner and buying directly from the lender. Your goal is to help them out of their foreclosure situation and find a great real estate investment for yourself.

CHAPTER 4

How to Find
Short-Sale Foreclosures

You can find short-sale foreclosure opportunities anywhere foreclosures are happening. In this chapter we
will teach you how to find foreclosures. You have to
be a pretty good detective if you are going to be a successful
real estate investor. You have to be a great detective if you are
going to be successful investing in foreclosures. What you are
looking for is the owner in distress.

We are going to give you the 13 key words or phrases
that we look for when we go through classified ads, work with
our personal contacts, do our own scouting, visit open houses,
or work with a real estate agent. When you see or hear one or
more of these words or phrases, you will know that you have
found the right owner.

Finding Properties in Preforeclosure

Finding properties before the notice of default occurs can be
difficult. There is no official public record available to you that
would alert you to a property owner's financial troubles. Instead
you have to search for clues to their financial troubles, being
proactive at seeking opportunities in the preforeclosure phase.

Clues to an owner in distress include deferred maintenance on a property or the look of a property being abandoned.

41

Other clues are general lack of care by the owner or tenant or frequent official deliveries of notices to pay.

It takes a keen eye to observe some of these subtle hints to a preforeclosure condition. Networking with neighbors and service providers such as delivery companies, utility providers, and postal carriers can provide you with extra eyes.

13 Key Words or Phrases

1. Must Sell

Any time you encounter the phrase *must sell,* you have come upon the right owner. It is perfectly acceptable to ask the must-sell owner why they must sell. You may discover that they are selling because they are behind on their mortgage payments.

We have heard some pretty strange reasons for selling as well as the fairly standard legitimate reasons for selling. The point is that an owner's must-sell reason is his or her own.

2. Under Market

The phrase *under market* can let you know that you have come upon the right owner and the right property. As a real estate investor you are a wholesale buyer. A property that is advertised as being under market puts you ahead of the game from the start.

Of course, you have to investigate to be able to determine if the owner really knows what they are talking about. *Under market* to a property owner may still mean the property is overpriced to you as a real estate investor.

3. Below Appraisal

Below appraisal is a phrase we like to hear. This occurs when a real estate agent tells us the property they are marketing for the owner is priced below the appraisal value. We know we have the right property and the right owner.

Again, you have to be careful here. Below what appraised value? Are we talking below the appraised value for insurance purposes? Are we talking below the appraised value for property tax purposes? Are we talking below the appraised value for a home equity loan? Or, are we talking below the appraised value for a recent market comparison? The last value is the only one that counts.

4. *Transferred*

Transferred can simply mean transferred. Or, transferred can be a code word for an owner in distress. In today's economy, when someone is transferred, they are often happy to have a job to be transferred to.

But they may have been out of a job for a while and be in preforeclosure. This can be a nightmare for the owner. You may be able to put together a very profitable deal and stop the owner's bad dream.

5. *Divorce*

When you see or hear the word *divorce,* there is often a real estate deal close by. There are 2 million to 3 million new marriages each year in the United States. There are 1 million to 1.5 million divorces. What happens to the family home when there is a divorce? Statistics tell us that most real estate in a divorce winds up being sold so that the assets can be divided between the ex-spouses.

We have found the best offers in a divorce-involved property are all cash offers. Each side is willing to take a hit on the purchase price because each wants as much of their equity in cash as possible. Sometimes we have been able to put a good deal together several months after the divorce when the property becomes too much for the remaining party to handle. We can relieve the divorced owner of their financial problem and make money for ourselves.

6. Foreclosure Ad

Usually, you see something like this in a real estate classified ad:

Owner in foreclosure.
  Bring all offers.
  3Br/2Ba $169,500
  Good area.
  (817) 555-2455

Call about the ad, identifying yourself as a real estate investor. Find out when the foreclosure sale is scheduled to occur. Set an appointment to meet with the owner to show them what foreclosure options they may have. Make an offer to buy their equity.

7. Illness Ad

Unfortunately, illness is a fact of life. Sometimes your job as a real estate investor can really help people out of a tough situation. A real estate ad we saw read something like this:

Illness forces sale.
  Great family home in good area.
  Priced to sell. $275,000.
  Call Jon. (972) 555-2455

We called Jon and found out that his wife had multiple sclerosis. They had a two-story home and Jon's wife could no longer climb the stairs. They were selling because they needed a one-story home and they needed money for medical bills. This was a preforeclosure waiting to happen.

8. Death

"Death forces sale." This was the heading of a classified ad we read one morning in our local newspaper. Pretty tough situation, but the widow needed to sell after her husband was killed in a traffic accident.

The notice of default had already been posted. We made an equity share offer on the property. We agreed to a price for today and split any future appreciation fifty-fifty. We would split the monthly payments fifty-fifty. That way she could stay in the property. Her problem was resolved and we got a good deal.

9. Owner Will Carry

When you see or hear *owner will carry,* you have found a built-in real estate lender to finance the deal. The owner is going to act as the lender. They are going to carry a mortgage or trust deed for part or all of the purchase price.

We have found that an owner in preforeclosure will offer to carry financing in order to make their property more attractive to more buyers. We have asked owners to carry the financing on our equity purchase in order to make the deal work.

10. Nothing Down

No down payment. Zero. Nada. *Nothing down* means an owner wants their property to be the most competitive one on the market. This can also be an indication that the owner does not have a lot of time because of an impending foreclosure.

The owner may just want someone to take over the loan payments and get on down the road. Of course, nothing down may just mean nothing down, and you still may be able to make some quick cash or get a great long-term wealth-building deal because of the great terms.

11. 100 Percent Financing

A variation of nothing down is *100 percent financing.* We may have a worried owner who has to sell the property and is willing to finance the sale rather than lose all his or her equity.

This is one of those phrases that we never pass up when we encounter it.

One thing to look out for when you see 100 percent financing is a property that will go with VA financing. This means the owner will cooperate with a VA buyer. Although there is no down payment for the VA buyer, this is not owner financing that you can use as a real estate investor.

12. Motivated Seller

A *motivated seller* is the right owner. As a real estate investor, you are looking for motivated sellers. Owners in preforeclosure are motivated sellers. A motivated seller might just give you the deed to their property and walk away!

It would be fair to say that all the owners with whom we have done business in the foreclosure arena are motivated. When we encounter an owner who is not motivated, we usually have a very hard time doing business with them.

13. Lost Job/Laid Off

The pink slip is an anachronism from the twentieth century when people actually got a pink slip to let them know that they were either fired or laid off. In the twenty-first-century economy, companies want fewer workers doing more work.

As a real estate investor, when you see *lost job* or *laid off* in a real estate ad or when one of your personal contacts alerts you about someone losing a job, more than likely there is a real estate deal to be made. It is a fact that most people live paycheck to paycheck. When they lose the paycheck, unfortunately, the family home may not be far behind.

So now you know 13 key words or phrases to look for. What proactive steps can you take to find good deals?

Advertise

Sometimes a well-placed advertisement in the newspaper or online or notices posted on public bulletin boards in supermarkets or business establishments can often place an inquisitive owner in contact with you in the preforeclosure stage. We have had continuing success with the following verbiage as a newspaper, bulletin board, or Internet ad.

MISSED YOUR PAYMENT AGAIN?

> Private party will share ways to save
> your home/protect your equity.
> Learn 8 ways to avoid foreclosure.
> Free! Call 817.555.1212

Searching the Public Record

There are two ways to search the public record to glean information about foreclosures or potential foreclosures. You can do it yourself, or you can pay a foreclosure service to provide you with the foreclosure information.

Do It Yourself

For most of you, the public records are at your local county courthouse. For some of you, the public records may be at your City Hall. More and more, you can access the public records through the Internet. The problem with checking the public records yourself is the tremendous amount of records there are to check.

Title insurance companies have to do a title search on a property before they will issue title insurance. This process can take several weeks. The title insurance company will issue a preliminary title report as a prelude to issuing a policy of title insurance.

We recommend you plan on an entire day to visit the county recorder's office for your county. You will probably find the public records section buried deep in the bowels of your county courthouse.

Ask for Help

Ask for help from the staff to direct you to the foreclosure postings for the current month. Once you have the legal description of the property from the foreclosure posting and the property owner's name, you can look up the property in the public record and also check for liens against the owner.

The property record will reflect any liens against the owner. If you are going to do business with a new buyer, you might also want to check the buyer out. For example, if you are going to flip a foreclosure property and carry back financing, this would be a good idea. Sometimes the new buyer will bring clouds to the property title because of liens associated with the buyers personally, such as IRS liens.

Brain Trust

Divorce is the number one cause of property foreclosures in this country. A Brain Trust hint for those of you who like being detectives is to follow the public record on filings for dissolution of marriage (the official term for divorce). Then make contact with property owners who are involved with the divorce. This may give you a head start on identifying properties that are headed down the foreclosure path.

Foreclosure Service

You can get information about foreclosures from a foreclosure service. A typical price may be $35 per month for the foreclosure list for your county. A typical price for the year may be $225. Shop around because there may be more than one foreclosure service in your area. You do not need anything fancy, just the basic information will do.

We recommend spending the money for a one-month copy. If you decide you like working foreclosures after the notice of default is posted and are going to get into it big time, then pay for the six-month or one-year subscription. If this is not the foreclosure phase you are interested in, then you have not spent too much money.

Foreclosure Letter

For some of you, face-to-face contact with strangers on a subject of such a sensitive nature as foreclosure may prove uncomfortable. Also, it may be tough for a property owner facing foreclosure to come to grips with their shame and embarrassment. For both of these reasons, a letter campaign may be a good method to consider in your pursuit of eligible properties.

Although nothing beats personal contact, a program of contacting owners in distress via mail is often the only way to reach owners who are difficult to find. They may be occupying the property but have an unlisted or disconnected telephone number. They may have vacated the property but left a forwarding address. Just as in the personal contact and telephone meetings, your letter should be honest, sincere, and offer the owner hope.

In addition to the letter, we want you to include a picture of the property, which will create a better impact for the owner. The picture will show the owner that you have a strong interest in the property. After all you came out to look at the property to take the picture! Make sure you keep a copy of the picture for your files should the property owner contact you at a later date.

The following is the letter we have used. You may want to consider using it. Change it to fit your style and needs. You will notice that this letter is not short and sweet. It is short and to the point. The purpose of your letter is to get the owner's attention and to have the owner contact you because they feel you can help them.

Dear Property Owner,

According to the public records, the loan on your property may be in trouble. We are writing to you with an offer to help. We are real estate investors who have studied the foreclosure process. We are familiar with the procedure and understand the many ways in which owners can halt the foreclosure and perhaps save their property and equity.

We have made it a practice to contact owners like yourself who have received official notice of a pending foreclosure. We believe we may be able to help you by providing information about your foreclosure options. Sometimes we find excellent investment opportunities when owners have decided that they no longer wish to keep their property.

Specifically, there are eight actions you can take when your home is in foreclosure. We would like to share these options with you *at no cost or obligation to you.* We do this to increase our chances for investment opportunities and at the same time have an opportunity to help some owners who would otherwise lose their properties.

Time is running out! We urge you to contact us today before any more of your hard-earned equity is lost forever. We can be reached by phone, e-mail, or letter. We will keep our conversation confidential. We hope we can provide you with the information you need to save your property. *DON'T WAIT!* Contact us today!

Chantal and Bill Carey
(817) 555-2614; chantalandbillcarey@yahoo.com
PO Box 274, Bedford, Texas 76095-0274

Veterans Affairs and Federal Housing Administration Foreclosures

You can find out about Department of Veterans Affairs (VA) and Federal Housing Administration (FHA) foreclosures from your local VA and Housing and Urban Development (HUD) offices. They will likely refer you to a list of VA- and FHA- approved real estate brokers in your area who are authorized to list and give access to VA and FHA real estate owned portfolios (REOs).

These properties are auctioned off to the highest net bidder. The highest net bidder is the bidder whose bid, after real estate commissions and expenses, generates the most cash to the VA or FHA. Incidentally, your bid must be submitted in writing through an approved real estate broker. These are sealed bids that are opened by the appropriate VA or FHA representatives on a designated date.

Federal National Mortgage Association/Fannie Mae

Fannie Mae is a stockholder-owned, congressionally chartered corporation. Its stock is traded on the New York Stock Exchange and other major exchanges. It is listed on the Standard and Poor's 500 Stock Price Index. By buying and selling VA, FHA, and conventional loans in the secondary mortgage market, Fannie Mae has become the largest real estate lender in the country.

Fannie Mae Foreclosures

As the largest real estate lender, Fannie Mae has its share of foreclosures. As a stock corporation, it is profit oriented and interested in minimizing losses. One method of doing so is the Fannie Mae Preforeclosure Sale program.

The result to real estate investors can be the purchase of property from potential borrowers in default at prices below the existing loan and with new loan terms better than terms available on the open market. This is done on a case-by-case basis.

Why would Fannie Mae be willing to do this? The answer is to minimize losses. It is expensive for Fannie Mae to foreclose on, maintain, and then remarket a portfolio of properties. If it can dispose of the properties in preforeclosure, before it takes them into its property portfolio, Fannie Mae can save money.

Suffice it to say that Fannie Mae is willing to pass on some of the money it saves to real estate investors who purchase property under this program. Some of you are going to make some quick cash doing this type of foreclosure investing. Others of you are going to acquire some great properties to hold on to for long-term wealth building.

The program is directed toward real estate agents as the contact source with defaulting borrowers, potential retail or wholesale buyers, and the lenders, including Fannie Mae. Just as with VA and FHA foreclosures, you have to discover who the real estate brokers are who are handling Fannie Mae properties. Whether Fannie Mae moves to a new program, it will always be a source of foreclosure opportunities. Once you have established contact with a Fannie Mae broker, he or she will be able to keep you informed on any changes.

Summary

Remember, you must identify a potential foreclosure before you can determine if there will be a short-sale foreclosure opportunity. You also do not want to look a gift horse in the mouth. If you can find a great preforeclosure deal working with an owner in distress, by all means go for it.

In Chapter 5, "Dealing with Owners in Financial Distress," we will teach you how to deal with owners. Most of you think that buying a foreclosure occurs at a foreclosure sale. We are going to show you how to buy foreclosures before, during, and after the foreclosure sale. The key to finding a great short-sale foreclosure is finding an owner in financial distress.

Dealing with Owners in
Financial Distress

In this chapter we will teach you how to deal with owners in financial distress. Most people think that buying a foreclosure must occur at a foreclosure sale. Foreclosure sales are usually conducted on the courthouse steps in the county in which the property is located.

At one of the recent courthouse foreclosure sales we attended, more than a thousand properties were being auctioned in one day! This was the number of foreclosure sales for our county for one month! It was a total and complete zoo. At least five hundred people were trying to figure out what to do, whom to talk to, and where to bid. We bought nothing that day.

We are going to start you out with a better idea. Let's talk to the property owner who is in financial distress. They may be headed down the road to a full-blown foreclosure sale on the courthouse steps. If we can identify these owners in distress early enough, we may be able to help them as we help ourselves.

The first thing we need is the owner's permission to talk to their lender. Although we may want to bypass the owner in order to do a short-sale deal with their lender, the lender will not talk to us without the owner's permission. You must get in front of the property owner to be able to make any type of foreclosure deal happen.

Owners in Financial Distress

There are two time periods to work with owners in financial distress. There is the period before the lender files a
notice of default at the county recorder's office, and there
is the period after the lender files a notice of default at the
county recorder's office but before the foreclosure sale
takes place.

If you are able to develop rapport with the owner, you
will have a good chance to help the owner in distress as well
as make a good deal for yourself. In the event you are unable
to make a deal with the owner to buy their equity because
they have no equity, you will have the inside track to making a
short-sale deal with their lender.

Before you can deal with the owner or their lender you
must know the true value of the property. You must prepare
a list of comparable properties in the target area that have
sold. These comparable sales will give you the evidence to
make a great foreclosure deal. This is true whether you are
buying the owner's equity or doing a short-sale with the
lender.

Knowing Value

Are you ready to become an expert in valuing real estate? We
are going to take you step by step through the knowledge
we have gained in our combined 50-plus years as real estate
investors valuing real estate. We will define the six values that
every real estate investor needs to know about property they
are investing in.

We will show you the three ways to value real estate that
are used by real estate appraisers. We will explain the four elements of real estate value. Then, we will reveal the four great
forces that influence real estate value. Finally, we will teach
you the seven ways to know value in your target area. This
next section is the key to your success.

The Six Values Every Real Estate Investor Needs to Know

Six values every real estate investor needs to know are the retail value, the wholesale value, the replacement value, the property tax value, the loan value, and the appraised value. Once you know these six values, you can feel confident and comfortable making any real estate investment.

1. *Retail value* is the value an end user, such as homeowner, places on a piece of real estate. The retail value tends to be the highest value of all the values placed on real estate.
2. *Wholesale value* is the value a real estate investor, like you, places on a piece of real estate. The wholesale value tends to be the lowest value of all the values placed on real estate.
3. *Replacement value* is the value insurance companies place on the improvements on a piece of real estate. The replacement value is determined by the cost approach to value.
4. *Property tax value* is the value the local property tax assessor places on a piece of property. The property tax value could be higher or lower than the retail value.
5. *Loan value* is the value a real estate lender, such as a bank or mortgage company, places on a piece of real estate. The loan value tends to vary as a percentage of the appraised value.
6. *Appraised value* is the value a real estate appraiser places on a piece of property. The appraised value is typically at or near the retail value.

You now know the six values of real estate. Let's move on to the ways to value real estate.

Three Ways to Value Real Estate

There are three ways to value real estate. They are the cost approach, the income approach, and the market comparison approach. These three approaches to value are used by professional real estate appraisers when they appraise a property. The appraiser will use one, two, or possibly all three of these valuation approaches.

Cost Approach

The Cost Approach consists of three parts. First, value the land. Second, value the improvements on the land, such as buildings, and add the value of the improvements to the value of the land. Third, determine the accrued depreciation of the improvements and subtract the accrued depreciation from the combined value of the land and improvements.

Cost Approach Example

Let's look at an example. If the land is valued at $100,000, the improvements are valued at $250,000, and the accrued depreciation is $25,000, what is the value of the property according to the cost approach?

Land Value	$100,000
Improvements	$250,000
Total	$350,000
Accrued Depreciation	−$25,000
Property Value	$325,000

We added the value of the improvements, $250,000, to the value of the land, $100,000, and got $350,000. We then subtracted the accrued depreciation, $25,000, and came up with a property value of $325,000.

Income Approach

The income approach uses the income a property produces to determine its value. We say it this way: The value of an income property is in direct relationship to the income the property produces.

There are two ways to determine value using the income approach. They are the gross rent multiplier and the formula *value = income ÷ capitalization rate.*

Gross Rent Multiplier

The gross rent multiplier says the value of an income-producing property is determined by the gross annual rent the property receives multiplied by the gross rent multiplier. You can find out the gross rent multiplier for your area by calling a commercial real estate company and asking them what the gross rent multiplier is for your area. If the gross annual rent is $120,000 and the gross rent multiplier for the area is 8, then we multiply $120,000 by 8 and come up with a value of $960,000.

Gross Rent	$120,000
Gross Rent Multiplier	×8
Value	$960,000

Formula

The other way to determine value using the income approach is with the formula *value = income ÷ capitalization rate.* In this case the income is the net operating income (NOI), which is the gross income minus the operating expenses. The capitalization rate is determined by the market in the area the property is located.

Capitalization Rate

For example, in Dallas, Texas, real estate investors might require an 8 percent capitalization rate, and in Phoenix, Arizona, real estate investors might require a 9 percent capitalization rate. You can find out the capitalization rate for your area by calling a commercial real estate company and asking them.

If the net operating income is $80,000 and the capitalization rate is 8 percent (Dallas, Texas), then the value of the property is $1,000,000 ($80,000 ÷ .08 = $1,000,000). However, if the property is located in Phoenix, Arizona, with the same $80,000 net operating income, then the value of the property is only $888,888 ($80,000 ÷ .09 = $888,888).

Dallas, Texas		Phoenix, Arizona
$80,000	Net Operating Income	$80,000
.08	Capitalization Rate	.09
$1,000,000	Property Value	$888,888

Market Comparison Approach

The market comparison approach uses the value of similar properties to determine the value of a particular property. How many of you have heard the term *comps*? Comps is short for "comparable properties." You compare properties that are similar to the property you are interested in to determine its value. Our rule of thumb is "No comps, no contract."

Market Comparison Example

Let's look at an example. If you are trying to determine the value of a three bedroom/two bathroom, 1,600 square feet, attached two-car garage home, you compare it to as similar properties as you can find in the neighborhood that have sold within the last 180 days.

Property 1 is a three bedroom/two bathroom, 1,625 square feet, attached two-car garage home that sold for $195,000 45 days ago. Property 2 is a three bedroom/two bathroom, 1,575 square feet, attached two-car garage home that sold for $190,000 60 days ago. Property 3 is a three bedroom/two bathroom, 1,700 square feet, attached two-car garage home that sold for $205,000 30 days ago.

The price per square foot for each of these properties is $120. The price per square foot is determined by dividing the price by the square footage ($195,000 ÷ 1,625 square feet is $120.00; $190,000 ÷ 1,575 square feet is $120.63; $205,000 ÷ 1,700 square feet is $120.59).

By inspecting these three prices per square foot we can see $120 per square foot would be a reasonable value to use. If the three prices per square foot were markedly different, then you could use the average of the three. If we multiply our 1,600 square feet times $120 we get a value of $192,000 for the value of the property we are looking at.

Property 1	**Property 2**	**Property 3**
$195,000	$190,000	$205,000
1,625	1,575	1,700
$120.00	$120.63	$120.59
Per Sq Ft	Per Sq Ft	Per Sq Ft

Subject Property

1,600 Square Feet
×$120.00 Per Sq Ft
$192,000

This, of course, is a summary chart of the market comparison example information. To help you determine the most accurate values of properties you are analyzing you may want to use a form to organize the information you gather.

When you understand these three approaches to valuing real estate, you will begin to think like a professional appraiser. When you are looking at a property, you will start thinking what approach to value makes the most sense in valuing that property. Next we cover the four elements of value.

Four Elements of Value

There are four elements of value in real estate. These four elements are demand, utility, scarcity, and transferability. These four elements of value constitute the value of a piece of real estate.

1. *Demand* is the number of people who want the property. The more people who want the property, the more valuable the property becomes.
2. *Utility* is the use that a property can be put to or made of. The more uses that a property can be put to or made of, the more valuable the property.
3. *Scarcity* has to do with the supply of real estate available. This supply could be what is on the market or the total possible number of properties in an area. The

scarcer the supply of real estate available, the more valuable the property.

4. *Transferability* is the key element of value in real estate. You may have the best property in the world, worth millions of dollars, but if you cannot transfer the title to your property, the property could become worthless. Likewise, if you are a real estate buyer and have written a great wholesale offer that has been accepted by the seller, your deal is worthless unless you can get the seller to transfer clear property title to you.

When you know the four elements of value, you have an advantage over your competition. You may be able to create a new demand for the property. You may see a use for a property that no one else sees. You could add a feature to the property that is not normally available. You may figure out a way to transfer a property title that other people cannot figure out. All of these will add value to the property. Now we turn our attention to the four great forces that influence value.

Four Great Forces Influencing Value

Four great forces influence the value of real estate. They are physical forces, economic forces, political forces, and social forces. These four great forces are present in every real estate market in the country. How they influence your target area is up to you to determine.

1. *Physical forces* are the availability of schools, shopping, churches, transportation, and parks. If these physical amenities are present in your target area, they influence the value of the area in an upward manner. If these physical amenities are not present or are minimally present in your target area, they influence the value of the area in a downward manner.

2. *Economic forces* are the number and types of jobs available, the wages paid, where in the economic cycle

the economy is nationally, and the interest rates for real estate loans. The economic cycle is a repeating expansion, prosperity, recession, depression cycle. Real estate value is greatly influenced by the economic cycle. Typically, real estate is said to do well in the expansion and prosperity phases of the economic cycle and poorly in the recession and depression phases of the economic cycle.

3. *Political forces* are the types of zoning, pro-growth or no-growth policies, and environmental regulations that influence the value of real estate. A zoning change can greatly affect the value of a piece of property. It is important for you to know the political forces that influence the value of real estate in your area, both for the present and future investment climate.

4. *Social forces* are the quality of the schools and the number in the area, blighted neighborhoods or well-kept neighborhoods, racial or ethnic strife, and social amenities such as museums, art galleries, and concert halls.

When you understand these four great forces you will have a sense of when and how the real estate market can change. Sometimes one great force will act alone and change the market. At other times several of the great forces will act simultaneously and change the market. Now we will show you how to know value in your target area.

Seven Ways to Know Value in Your Target Area

There are seven ways to know value in your target area. They include sold comparables, pending comparables, listed comparables, expired comparables, appreciation rates, new or planned developments, and vacancy rates. The first five of these can be obtained from your local real estate brokers. The last two can be obtained from the local planning commission and the apartment owner's association.

1. *Sold comparables* are comparable properties that have been sold and have actually closed escrow. Sold comparables set the floor of retail value for real estate. This means that if a sold comparable sold for $125,000, a similar property should sell for no less than $125,000 in a normal real estate market. Sold comparables are useful for properties that have sold in the last six months. Anything beyond six months is not considered a good sold comparable.

2. *Pending comparables* are properties that have sold but that have not closed escrow. Pending comparables indicate the direction of real estate value. When the pending comparables close escrow they become a sold comparable. If the sold comparables are indicating a value of $125,000 and the pending comparables are indicating a value of $127,000, then you have an indication that the direction of real estate values is going up.

3. *Listed comparables* are properties currently on the market and similar to the property in which you are considering investing. Listed comparables set the ceiling of retail value for real estate because they have neither sold nor closed escrow. They are merely an indicator of what sellers would like to get for their properties.

4. *Expired comparables* are properties that never sold let alone closed escrow. They are expired listings that indicate the value that is beyond the present market in terms of what retail real estate buyers are willing to pay for property. Retail buyers will buy the lower-priced comparable properties first, all things being equal.

5. *Appreciation rates* indicate the annual percentage increases in market value. Appreciation rates give you a sense of how hot or cold the real estate market is. Double-digit appreciation rates indicate a hot real estate market. Single-digit appreciation rates indicate a good real estate market. Zero or negative appreciation rates indicate a cold real estate market.

6. *New or planned developments* indicate the path of development in your area. When you are able to buy property in the path of that development, you are helping to insure that you are buying property that will appreciate in value. This is important when you are using the quick cash strategy and flipping property to a long-term wealth-building investor. It will also benefit you if you are using a long-term wealth-building strategy.

7. *Vacancy rates* indicate an area's potential or problems. Low vacancy rates indicate an area that may have profitable properties. High vacancy rates indicate an area that may have problem properties. You may want to do more research to find out if the vacancy rates reflect the historical trend.

We are going to conclude this training on real estate value with the final four pieces of the value puzzle. We are going to teach you about the principle of progression, median price, average price, and the principle of regression.

The Final Four

The economic *principle of progression* as it relates to real estate investing says that if you buy a property below the median price for the area, there will be a positive impact on the future value of that property just because of the area itself. Another way to say this is that when you buy a property that is priced below the median price, there are more properties priced at a higher level than are priced at a lower level relative to the property you are buying.

First of all, let's figure out what the *median price* means. The median price is the price at which half of the property in the area is more expensive and half of the property is less expensive. The median price is different from the average price. The *average price* is higher than the median price and is skewed that way because of the expensive property in an area.

As we have already said, the median price is the price at which half of the properties in an area are more expensive and half of the properties in an area are less expensive. We know that the market comparison approach to value places the most emphasis on sold comparable properties. The median price takes all properties, not just comparable properties, into account. Let's look at five properties in the same neighborhood that have sold and closed escrow in the last six months.

Five Properties

Property 1 is a three bedroom, two bathroom, 1,200 square feet starter home that sold for $105,000. Property 2 is a four bedroom, two bathroom, 1,500 square feet older home that sold for $120,000. Property 3 is a four bedroom, two bathroom, 2,000 square feet newer home that sold for $155,000. Property 4 is a three bedroom, two bathroom, 1,800 square feet upgraded home that sold for $180,000. Property 5 is a five bedroom, four bathroom, 3,500 square feet executive home that sold for $290,000.

Median Price

What is the median price for these five properties? The answer may surprise you. The median price is $155,000, which is the price for which property 3 sold. Remember the median price is the price at which half of the properties sell for a higher price (properties 4 and 5) and half of the properties sell for a lower price (properties 1 and 2).

Average Price

What is the average price for these five properties? Again, the answer may surprise you. The average price for these five properties is $170,000! You can see that the average price is $15,000 higher than the median price ($170,000 versus $155,000). Property 4 and especially property 5, with their higher sales prices of $180,000 and $290,000, respectively, skew the average price higher. As a real estate investor you are much more interested in the median price.

Average Price versus Median Price

Average Price		Median Price	
Property 1	$105,000	Property 1	$105,000
Property 2	$120,000	Property 2	$120,000
Property 3	$155,000	Property 3	$155,000
Property 4	$180,000	Property 4	$180,000
Property 5	$290,000	Property 5	$290,000
Average Price = $170,000		Median Price = $155,000	

The economic *principle of regression* as it relates to real estate investing says that if you buy a property higher than the median price for the area, there will be a negative impact on the future value of that property just because of the area itself. Another way to say this is that when you buy a property that is priced above the median, there are more properties priced at a lower level than are priced at a higher level relative to the property you are buying.

Using our previous property examples, if you had purchased property 4 for $180,000, the value of that property for investment purposes would be negatively impacted by the principle of regression. Properties 1, 2, and 3, selling at or below the median price of $155,000, would all be pulling down the value of your property. Only property 5, selling at $290,000, would be pulling up the value of your property.

Now that you understand the final four pieces of the value puzzle, let's move further into dealing with owners in financial distress. The next thing you need to do is set an appointment with the owner.

Setting an Appointment with the Owner

When setting an appointment with the owner for the foreclosure presentation, plan to make only one presentation per evening. This is important because some owners will take longer to make a decision than others. If you have planned appointments too close together, each one will be rushed, and opportunities to acquire properties may be missed.

No appointment should be set unless all owners will be present. If you get to the appointment and one of the owners cannot be present, reschedule for another time. Otherwise, you are wasting your time.

It is important that the owner feels relaxed and is able to discuss their situation with you at the stated time. Accordingly, as with any real estate contract presentation, the time for the appointment should be at an hour when distractions such as kids and favorite TV shows are not competition.

Let's turn our attention to your initial phone conversation with the owner. The purpose of the conversation is to set an appointment with the owner. At this appointment you will make the foreclosure options presentation.

Phone Appointment Script

Hello, my name is _____ and I am calling because I may have an interest in buying your property. Are you the owner? What is your name?

Wait for their response. If they are not the owner, ask to speak to the owner.

According to public records, I understand that your loan may be in trouble and that you might be able to use some help. Is this a convenient time to talk?

Wait for their response. If they say no, ask when would be a good time for you to call back?

As I said, my name is _____ and I am a private real estate investor who makes it my practice to understand the foreclosure process and how to avoid it. My interest in your property stems from the fact that I can often find a good investment by talking to people who have a problem loan.

I sometimes find that they have a desire to sell their property at a price that will save some of their equity and help them protect their credit, and, at the same time, I may find a property to acquire.

I have developed a presentation that will show you your many options to avoid foreclosure. I recognize that nearly nine out of 10 owners will be able to save their property with this information.

I am willing to share this information with you without cost or obligation. The properties I do buy have made it worth my time to help many property owners such as yourself avoid foreclosure entirely. Do you have an interest in finding out about the eight options you have with regard to your pending foreclosure?

At this point you have aroused the curiosity of the owner, and setting the time for an appointment should be almost automatic.

I have time on my schedule tonight or tomorrow night. Because time is of the essence for some of these foreclosure options, would tonight or tomorrow night be better for you?

Wait for their response.

Would seven o'clock or eight o'clock be better for you?

Wait for their response. After you have set a time ask this last question.

Do you have younger children at home?

Wait for their response. If the say they have younger children say:

I recognize that it is important that parents spend quality time with their children, and I do not wish to disturb that. Is there a time, perhaps after your children have gone to bed, that we can talk?

Such consideration on your part will make an impression on the owner, show great respect for their family, and assure you of an uninterrupted appointment.

At the Appointment

Dress appropriately for the meeting. Do not overdress or arrive in too fancy a vehicle. Have a calm demeanor. Do not seem overly anxious to make a deal. Treat the owner with respect, diplomacy, and understanding. Listen more than you talk.

Take the time to develop rapport before you get into your questions. Be prepared to discuss details with the owner that will make it clear what the owner needs financially. In other words, discover the owner's true motivation and needs. Ask the questions in a friendly manner.

Inspect the Property

Ask the owner to show you around the property. Take notice of faulty conditions or red flags, which may indicate problems with the property. Use a clipboard and write your observations down. This will serve as a memory aid for you. It will also show the owner that you are serious about the property.

Avoid Making Any Proposals

There are no oral agreements in real estate. At this initial meeting you are gathering information about the owner and the property and making your presentation. Any proposal you make should be in writing and done when all the decision makers are present. This may occur immediately after you have finished your foreclosure presentation. It could also be done at your next appointment.

Use a Foreclosure Options Presentation

For best results, follow a written outline in discussing the owner's options. Your goals are to have the owner understand the foreclosure process, clearly see his options, recognize your knowledge of the subject, and put together a mutually beneficial contract.

At the Foreclosure Options Presentation

Your purpose at the foreclosure options presentation is to create a mutually beneficial solution to the foreclosure problem for you and the property owner. After no more than five minutes of chitchat during which you are building rapport with the owner, you should begin your foreclosure options presentation at the owner's dining table.

We recommend you sit with your back to an outside wall. That way the owner(s) are giving you their full attention and will not be distracted by what is going on in the rest of the house. Please ask that TV or loud music that can be heard from the table be turned off or down.

Ask questions first. Expand on your knowledge of the owner's situation. Make sure you understand the owner's situation completely before you propose any solutions to their foreclosure problem. Then make your foreclosure options presentation.

Foreclosure Options

The eight foreclosure options are renegotiate, reinstate, or redeem the loan, give a deed in lieu of foreclosure to the lender, seek a legal delay, file for bankruptcy protection, sell the property, or do nothing. Some of these foreclosure options are time sensitive. Others require an expenditure of money that the owner probably does not have.

By analyzing the owner's situation, you can determine the best solution. If they have the ability to get their hands on some money, the owner may be able to renegotiate, reinstate, or redeem their loan with the lender. The owner can deed the property to the lender. If they want to hire an attorney, they may seek a legal delay or file bankruptcy. If they have enough time, the owner may be able to sell the property. If the owner does nothing, they will lose the property at the foreclosure sale.

Foreclosure Solutions

You are the solution to the owner's foreclosure problem. Let's assume the owner has neither the money nor the time to make something positive happen on their own with the information you have shared with them. This is where you step in and propose some very creative solutions.

The simplest solution is for you to buy the owner's equity. Of course, this assumes that the owner has equity to buy. If the owner does not have equity in the property, then you propose doing a short-sale with the owner and the lender. Let's look at an example in which the owner does have equity in the property.

Buy the Equity Example

Let's say the property is worth $210,000. The loan balance is $150,000. The owner is behind $12,000 in payments. The owner's remaining equity position is $48,000. You want to make an offer to buy the owner's $48,000 of remaining equity.

Owner's Equity

Property Value	$210,000
Loan Balance	−$150,000
Gross Equity	$60,000
Behind in Payments	−$12,000
Owner's Remaining Equity	$48,000

You offer the owner $11,000 for their remaining equity. They accept your offer. The owner would give you a quit-claim deed to the property. You, or the new buyer, will have to come up with an additional $12,000 to reinstate the loan. You would be paying $173,000 for the property. If the property has a value of $210,000, this looks like you have $37,000 in equity.

Purchase Price

Loan Balance	$150,000
Behind in Payments	$12,000
Equity Offer	+$11,000
Purchase Price	$173,000

It is now time to turn our attention to when to buy short-sale foreclosures. You can make a short-sale deal with the owner and the lender before the foreclosure sale up to and including the day of the foreclosure sale. You can even get a short-sale price from the lender after the lender forecloses on the property. Your course of action depends on your investment goals and the opportunities available.

CHAPTER 6

When to Buy Short-Sale Foreclosures

In this chapter we are going to show you when to buy short-sale foreclosures. You may buy short-sale foreclosures before, during, or after the foreclosure sale. It is up to you when to get involved in the real estate foreclosure market. This will depend on how much cash you have to invest and whether you have a quick cash or long-term wealth-building strategy.

In our book *The New Path to Real Estate Wealth: Earning without Owning*, we emphasize flipping the paperwork of real estate to make quick cash. In most short-sale situations, you must buy the property and close on it before you can flip it. You cannot just flip your short-sale contract. In Chapter 19, "Flipping Your Short-Sales," we will show you how to flip your short-sales for a quick profit.

Timing the Foreclosure Buy

In situations in which a property owner is in financial distress and their property is headed to a foreclosure sale, there are four distinct time periods in which you have an opportunity to acquire the property. Each of these time periods has benefits and drawbacks.

These four time periods are (1) before the notice of default is filed or posted at the county courthouse, (2) after

73

the notice of default is filed or posted at the county court-house, (3) during the foreclosure sale, and (4) after the foreclo-sure sale when the property belongs to a new owner who is either the foreclosing lender or another real estate investor.

As an example, let's see at what points the four time peri-ods or phases occur on the Texas foreclosure timeline. This will help you to identify the four time periods on your area's foreclosure timeline. We will then discuss each phase of the foreclosure timeline.

Texas Foreclosure Timeline

2–3 Months	20 days		Can Be 1 Day	21 Days Minimum
No Payments	1st	2nd	Posting	Sale
	Official	Official	at	1st
	Letter	Letter	Courthouse	Tuesday

Phase 1: Before the Posting of the Notice of Default

Whether the posting is called a notice of default in the case of a deed of trust or a *lis pendens* in the case of a mortgage, this marks the official beginning of the foreclosure. Once the foreclosure process begins, it may lead to the forced sale of the owner's property, the loss of their equity, and the resulting damage to their credit.

If you can make a deal with the owner before the com-mencement of legal action, you will help the owner to reduce the negative effects of foreclosure. You may also find that you can obtain a better buy because there will be less competition from other real estate investors for the property prior to the public notice of default or the *lis pendens* being recorded at the county recorder's office.

The drawback with trying to make a deal in this time period is you may find that the owner is not as motivated as they will be in the next time periods. We have found that own-ers at this point are still clinging to the unrealistic hope that a financial miracle is going to happen.

Using the Texas foreclosure timeline, this is the period up to the posting of the notice of default at the county courthouse. The owner is several months behind in their payments. Their lender may have already sent them a warning letter. The owner is starting to feel some pressure. Your job is to show them that the pressure is only going to get more intense. If the owner acts now with you, the pressure will dissipate and they will have an early resolution to their problem.

Early Resolution

Few borrowers intend to default on their loans. Sometimes economic developments beyond their control can create the situations leading to foreclosure. They may have been fired from their job. Their job may have disappeared. Interest rates may have increased on their adjustable rate mortgage and made their mortgage payments prohibitive.

Divorce, premature death, disability, illness, addiction, and accident can all lead to foreclosure. Poor money management, such as too much money in the stock market, can be a recipe for financial disaster. The result of the foreclosure can be embarrassing to the borrower, besides suffering the devastating financial consequences of losing their property and equity.

Early resolution of the pending foreclosure benefits the borrower and can produce better results for you as the real estate investor. Additionally, completing a transaction before the foreclosure period begins (once the posting occurs) can often avoid specific legislative guidelines that become restrictive on certain transactions. Of course, if the early resolution is not taken advantage of, the borrowers then find themselves in the situation of the notice of default being posted.

Phase 2: After the Posting of the Notice of Default

Once the notice of default has been posted, you must consider a number of things. First, your individual area may enforce certain restrictions and legal requirements when a property is officially in foreclosure. Second, once the notice of default is recorded, there is public knowledge of the default, and you will find you have competition from other real estate investors for the property.

Using the Texas foreclosure timeline, this is the period after the posting of the notice of default and before the actual foreclosure sale. This can be a period as short as 21 days in Texas. Check with a title insurance company to find out what the time period is in your area As we said, some areas may have legislative requirements an investor must follow once the notice of default has been recorded. We will use California as an example.

Legislative Requirements

In California, once the notice of default is posted at the courthouse, you, as the real estate investor, must comply with several state laws. These laws were enacted by the California legislature to protect homeowners from real estate investor sharks.

Unfortunately, as with many well-intentioned laws, this law has had unintentional negative effects. It has inhibited defaulting homeowners from being able to sell their homes to legitimate real estate investors who are trying to create a win-win situation for the defaulting homeowners and themselves. Yes, it may protect some defaulting homeowners from unscrupulous people, but it puts onerous restrictions on homeowners' property rights. Take a look at the California foreclosure timeline.

California Foreclosure Timeline

2–3 Months	3–4 Weeks		3 Months	20 Days	Next Day
No Payments	1st Official Letter	2nd Official Letter	Posting at Courthouse	Redeem Only	Sale

In California, if you are buying a property that is occupied by the owner, is a single-family residence up to a fourplex, and a notice of default has been posted against the property, you must include in your real estate purchase contract two notices required by California law.

You must include a five-day cancellation of contract notice and a notice informing the homeowner that they cannot be asked to sign a deed transferring title to their property to you until the five-day cancellation of contract period expires. If you do not do this, the homeowner can come back against you and have the courts void your deal and impose fines and penalties against you.

Notice Required by California Law

Until your right to cancel this contract has ended _____ (buyer) or anyone working for _____ (buyer) CANNOT ask you to sign or have you sign any deed or any other document. You may cancel this contract for the sale of your house without any penalty or obligation at any time before ____ (A.M./P.M.) on _____, 20__. See the attached notice of cancellation form for an explanation of this right.

NOTICE OF CANCELLATION
_____

(Enter date contract signed)

You may cancel this contract for the sale of your house, without penalty or obligation, at any time before _____.
To cancel this transaction, personally deliver a signed and dated copy of this cancellation notice, or send a telegram to _____ (buyer) at _____ (address)
NOT LATER THAN _____.
I hereby cancel this transaction_____ (date)

_____

_____

(Sellers' signatures)

Benefits and Drawbacks of the Notice of Default

One benefit of the notice of default is the sense of urgency it creates for the property owner. Once the foreclosure process has begun, it is only a matter of time before the property will be sold to the highest bidder. Coupled with the ever-shrinking equity that remains for the owner as time goes by, you can often make a good investment if you can get in touch with the owner during this time period.

Of course, every other real estate investor who follows the notice of default postings is now aware of these properties. This can be a huge drawback to you as you now are competing with many other investors for the same properties.

You can turn this potential drawback into an advantage, however, once you get in front of the owner and make your foreclosure options presentation. The owner's best option is to sell their equity to you. If they have no equity, the owner's best option is to agree to do a short-sale with you.

Once most investors find out the owner has no equity, they will be unwilling and unable to put together a mutually beneficial deal. With your willingness and ability to put together a short-sale, you are way ahead of the competition. No one else will be interested in helping the owner like you are.

Phase 3: At the Sale

For those of you who wait until the day of the foreclosure sale to get involved, preparation is of the utmost importance. The time you spend in researching both the property and the title will pay huge dividends when you are bidding. Again, we reiterate that you must know value before you make any bids.

We suggest you attend several foreclosure sales as dry runs to get a sense of how things occur, especially with regard to the trustees conducting the sales. Perhaps even more important is going to foreclosure sales to observe your competition before you actually start bidding.

While at the foreclosure sales, observe the habits of the successful bidders. Some of these faces you will see again and again. Note their habits and what they do when they enter the bidding.

On properties a bidder wants, do they enter the bidding at the beginning, middle, or end? Are some of the bidders working together to squeeze out the competition? Also take note of what a bidder does when he or she folds.

The advantage of buying at the foreclosure sale is the finality of it. You will receive your money back if the owner can exercise their right of redemption. All junior liens will be wiped out. You have the protection of your area's foreclosure laws for the winning bidder. It is a can't-lose proposition for you, and you have an upside potential because you bought the property wholesale.

The big disadvantage to buying at the foreclosure sale is that you have to pay cash. This may be up to 50 percent more cash than doing a short-sale. The other disadvantage is the sheer number of other investors you may encounter at the foreclosure sale who want to bid on or buy the properties you are interested in. Let's look at what happens if the property does not sell.

Phase 4: After the Foreclosure Sale

When a property does not sell at the foreclosure sale, the lender will take it back. There are two types of lenders: institutional lenders and private lenders. If the lender is an institutional lender, the property will become real estate owned (REO). Lenders are anxious to liquidate these properties. Because they are not in the real estate resale business, however, lenders sometimes mishandle these properties.

To find out about a lender's REOs, do not rely on the branch manager of a bank for much help. REOs are kept quiet, and it will take some probing to discover these potential pearls.

Your best source for REOs may be a real estate agent who handles them in your area. An agent may specialize in REO properties and have useful contacts already in place with several lenders. Do some calling around to find out who these real estate agents are.

If you have no other contact, establish a rapport with the branch manager of your bank or savings association. Ask the manager to make an introductory call to the REO manager. This manner of making the appointment will give you a personal introduction to the person in charge of the bank's REOs. You will not have to waste your time going up the food chain over the phone.

Private REOs

What if the lender who winds up with the property after the foreclosure sale is a private lender? They may have even less motivation to own the property than the institutional lenders. Typically, these lenders were owners of the property in the past. They sold the property and helped the buyer with seller carry-back financing in order to make the deal work.

The private lender may not want to take the time to remarket the property and may have moved out of the area. What about the expenses of holding the property while the lender resells it? The private lender certainly does not want to have to find a tenant and become a landlord. They may have gotten back title to the property, have no money in their pockets, and be facing the prospect of having to make payments on an existing senior lien. This can make private lenders extremely motivated to make a deal.

We recommend you talk to the lender or the lender's representative immediately after the foreclosure sale. Some of you may find your foreclosure-investing niche working exclusively with REO private lenders. Remember, they have made a credit bid for the amount of their loan balance, plus the back payments, plus foreclosure expenses, plus payments on the senior lien. If no one bids, the lender gets the title to the property. The lender may sell their position to you for a lot less than their credit bid once they wind up with the property. Let's look at some numbers.

Let's say the lender is in a second position with a $25,000 loan balance, $1,250 in back payments, $750 in foreclosure expenses, and five months of payments on the senior lien of $4,000.

Credit Bid

Loan Balance	$25,000
Back Payments	$1,250
Foreclosure Expenses	$750
Senior Lien Payments	+$4,000
Credit Bid	$31,000

No one has bid above the $31,000 credit bid. You may be able to offer $15,000 cash and have the lender give you title to the property. Do you think that may be a good deal? Our answer is that it depends.

What is the value of the property? What is the amount of the senior lien? Are there other liens against the title that you will be stuck with once you have the title to the property?

Our point is that just because you are getting what looks like a good deal from the private REO lender, as with all foreclosure deals, caveat emptor—let the buyer beware! You still have to do your due diligence and know about the property and the condition of the title before you make an investment.

Another Real Estate Investor

You may find you are able to make a deal with the real estate investor who makes the successful winning bid at the foreclosure sale. This investor may be buying the property with a plan to fix it up and put it back on the market. You did not bid higher during the auction because you had reached your predetermined top bid, but you already have a buyer who will pay $10,000 more than the winning bid.

You could offer the other real estate investor $5,000 more than they paid to sell you the property on the spot. Although they may have a profitable plan for the property, they may sell you the property for the immediate $5,000 profit. You would then flip the property to your buyer and make your own $5,000 profit.

Summary

There are four time periods or phases to invest in foreclosures. Although the foreclosure timeline varies from place to place, every area's foreclosure process includes these time periods.

These four time periods are before the notice of default is filed or posted at the county courthouse, after the notice of default is filed or posted at the county courthouse, during the foreclosure sale, and after the foreclosure sale when the property belongs to a new owner who is either the foreclosing lender or another real estate investor.

You can make quick cash or build long-term wealth in short-sale foreclosures no matter during which phase you make your investment. The key is to find your niche. Your niche is where you feel the most comfortable and confident. Your niche is also where you consistently make money. As you are getting started, try to make something happen in each foreclosure phase and discover for yourself where you belong.

Of course, our focus here is to show you how to access the real estate foreclosure market through the short-sale route. In the next chapter we will teach you how to create equity in the property even when the property owner has no equity. This is where you will learn to make a short-sale foreclosure deal when 99 percent of the other real estate investors cannot see any deal to be made.

CHAPTER 7

No Equity? No Problem!

Y ou can create equity in a property even when the owner has no equity. First we will talk about the owner who has equity in the property. Then we will talk about the owner who has no equity. Once you have made the foreclosure options presentation, ask the owner some additional questions. Your intention is really to help the owner make a decision. Because time really is of the essence for the owner, having them make a decision is in their best interest. You are doing them a disservice if you allow them to sell you the "they want to think about it" line.

It has been our experience that when people say they want to think about it, they never do. We have nothing against people wanting to think about it, we just know that typically people use "want to think about it" as a way to procrastinate. There is no time to procrastinate in the foreclosure arena.

Additional Questions

We ask the owner three additional questions.

1. Which of the foreclosure options does the owner think makes the most sense for their situation?

If the owner answers that they want to sell the property, we offer to buy their property. If the owner answers with anything other than they want to sell the property, we ask the next question.

2. Does the owner have the time and financial resources to carry out the foreclosure option they think makes the most sense?

If the owner cannot answer yes to both the time portion and the financial resources portion of the question, we let them know that particular foreclosure option is not going to work. We then offer to buy their property. If the owner answers yes to both the time and financial resources portions of the question, we ask them the next question.

3. Does the owner want our assistance in carrying out the foreclosure option they have decided on?

You have to be careful here. You cannot give the owner legal advice unless you are an attorney. You do not want to get too involved because you open yourself up to liability if things do not work out well for the owner, nor can you waste your time helping them without making any money.

When the owner says yes, they want our assistance; we have found that what works best for us is giving the owner the names of several attorneys that specialize in helping people in foreclosure. We leave the owner our contact information and keep open the possibility that we will buy their property.

When the owner says no, they do not want our assistance; we have found that what works best for us is leaving the owner our contact information and keeping open the possibility that we will buy their property. In other words, we are flexible knowing the owner may indeed call us back and offer to sell us their property.

The Owner Wants to Sell You Their Property

You have an owner who wants to sell you their property. The owner has equity in the property. What do you offer the owner for their property? You must make your offer based on your analysis of value. You are an investor buying at a wholesale price. As an investor, you cannot pay a retail price. Make your offer low and let the owner decide whether they will accept.

How do you know that you are buying at a wholesale price? You know you are buying at a wholesale price because you know value. You are an expert in valuing real estate in your investment target area. You know the retail value, the wholesale value, the appraised value, the loan value, the replacement value, and the property tax value of every property in which you are investing.

Buy the Owner's Equity, Not Their Property

We have an owner who is in the foreclosure process and wants to make a deal. What do we want to buy? Do we want to buy their equity, or do we want to buy their property? Our guideline is we want to buy the owner's equity if they have at least a 15 percent equity position in the property. We want to buy the owner's property through a short-sale if they have less than a 15 percent equity position in the property.

What Is Owner's Equity?

The owner's equity is the difference between the value of their property and any monetary liens or encumbrances against the owner's title to the property. If an owner owns a property free and clear, the owner's equity equals the value of the property.

Because the owner we are dealing with is in foreclosure, there is a monetary lien in the form of a mortgage or trust deed against the owner's title to the property. Their equity is the value of the property minus the mortgage balance minus the back payments minus any foreclosure expenses that have already accumulated.

In a nonforeclosure situation, if the retail value of the property is $200,000 and the mortgage balance against the property is $140,000, the owner's equity is $60,000.

Nonforeclosure Situation

Retail Value	$200,000
Mortgage	$140,000
Owner's Equity	$60,000

In a foreclosure situation, the value of a property is usually no longer the retail value. This may be for several reasons. The property may be run-down, the owner does not have the luxury of a normal marketing time to bring in the highest price, or the market may have turned downward. Typically, the value of the property is lowered automatically in a foreclosure situation. Let's say the value of the property is now $185,000 to $190,000.

The mortgage lien goes up in a foreclosure situation. The missed payments are added to the remaining balance of the mortgage. If the owner is behind in their payments $10,000, then the mortgage lien is now $150,000.

If the lender has formally initiated the foreclosure process, there are foreclosure expenses added to the mortgage balance. Now the owner's equity could be substantially reduced.

Foreclosure Situation

Foreclosure Value	$185,000
Behind in Payments	$10,000
Mortgage	−$140,000
Owner's Equity	$35,000

Your Offer

Instead of the owner's equity being $60,000 in the nonforeclosure situation, the owner's equity is $35,000 in the foreclosure situation. The owner has suffered a $25,000 loss in equity.

Please be clear about what we are saying here. The owner has suffered the equity loss. With a new owner in control of the property, the value of the property goes back up. The new owner will correct the run-down condition of the property. They have the ability to hold the property through a normal marketing time or until the market itself goes back up. As the value of the property increases, the owner's equity increases dollar for dollar.

Let's say you are going to offer the owner $10,000 for their $35,000 equity. If you keep the property, you are going to have to pay the lender the $10,000 in back payments to stop the foreclosure. Now you will have $20,000 in the property. If you must make repairs and do fix-up, you may have $3,000 to $5,000 more involved.

Then you add in mortgage payments, property tax payments, and insurance payments. Resale costs could add another $5,000 to $10,000 or more to your investment. When you add this all up, your total is $30,000 to $35,000!

Your Offer

Cash to Owner	$10,000
Cash to Lender	$10,000
Repairs and Fix-up	$5,000
Carrying and Resale Costs	$10,000
Total Invested	$35,000

This becomes a negotiating tool for you with the owner. Your point with the owner is that the maximum you can offer them is $10,000 cash for their equity. By giving the owner $10,000 for their equity, you will have $35,000 in the property before you make any money!

We have found that when we show the owner these types of figures they are much more amenable to accepting our offer. We are not trying to be mean to them or take advantage of them. We are trying to help them. But we (you) cannot help them if we (you) cannot make any money. Otherwise, we (you) will be in a foreclosure situation ourselves!

Making Money

Speaking of making money, let's look at the numbers. The mortgage balance is back to $140,000 (actually a little lower because the back payments reduced the principal, but really not worth mentioning). The property restored to retail value is now worth $200,000 (or perhaps a bit more).

If we sell the property to a retail buyer, we will make a $60,000 gross profit minus the $35,000 invested, equaling a $25,000 net profit. That is a 70 percent return over perhaps a three-month to six-month time period. That makes the investment worth the risk.

If we flip the contract to a real estate investor, we will have no cash to the owner, no cash to the lender, no repairs and fix-up costs, and no carrying and resale costs. Do you think it is possible to flip our contract for $5,000 to $10,000? What is the percentage return on our invested money? Did you say infinite?

Making Money

Sell to Retail Buyer		*Flip to Investor*	
Sales Price	$200,000	Flip Profit	$10,000
Mortgage	−$140,000	Mortgage	−0
Gross Profit	$60,000	Gross Profit	$10,000
Invested Money	−$35,000	Invested Money	−0
Net Profit	$25,000	Net Profit	$10,000

In Chapter 10, "Buying from the Lender before the Foreclosure Sale," we will show you how to negotiate with the property owner's lender. Success in these negotiations can benefit you and the owner. We will devote Chapter 16, "Buying from the Lender after the Foreclosure Sale," to negotiating with the lender after the foreclosure sale takes place.

No Equity? No Problem

What if the owner has no equity in the property? In this case, the short-sale foreclosure option comes into play. Using a short-sale you can create equity in the property even if the owner has no equity.

Let's say a borrower is three months behind on their $1,200 monthly mortgage payment. The amount outstanding on their loan is \$200,000. The lender is about to foreclose. The lender would like to receive the \$200,000 loan balance plus \$3,600 for the three back payments.

Loan Balance	\$200,000
Back Payments	+\$3,600
Lender Desired Payoff	\$203,600

Let's say the property is worth \$210,000. The owner has little or no equity in the property.

Property Value	\$210,000
Lender Desired Payoff	−\$203,600
Owner's Equity	\$6,400

Subtracting the typical 7 percent to 8 percent in closing costs, which is an additional \$14,000 to \$16,000 if the owner were to sell the property, would leave the owner having to put money into the deal!

Owner's Equity	\$6,400
Closing Costs	−\$16,000
Additional Owner Money	\$9,600

As a real estate investor, it also appears that there is no way for you to make money in this situation. Your competition thinks there is no way to make money on this deal. Actually, because there is no equity in the property, you have no competition. We have found that 95 percent to 99 percent of your competition has already walked away.

We are going to show you how to negotiate with the lender so that the lender will accept a reduced or short-sale loan payoff. Let's say you offer the lender \$169,000 for the property. If the lender accepts your offer you will have an instant \$41,000 equity position!

Property Value	\$210,000
Negotiated Lender Payoff	−\$169,000
Your Equity	\$41,000

Negotiating with the Lender

Why would the lender accept your $169,000 loan payoff offer? Because it is in the lender's best interest to do so! Let's look at the numbers from the lender's perspective.

If the lender goes through the foreclosure process and no one bids at the foreclosure sale because it looks like there is no equity in the property, the lender still has all the foreclosure costs. These costs include posting a notice of foreclosure and advertising the foreclosure sale. The lender will have to pay attorney's fees and trustee's fees. There are the day-of-sale foreclosure expenses they will have to pay. The lender will also have to pay for title insurance. The list goes on. The total could easily be $3,000 to $4,000.

After the lender takes back the property, they have additional expenses. The lender has to pay for repairs and fix-up costs, ongoing maintenance, hazard insurance and property taxes, and human resources costs. Let's call these costs holding costs. Again, the list goes on. This could easily amount to another $5,000 to $6,000.

Finally, the lender will have to put the property on the market for sale. The lender will have the closing costs and real estate commissions to pay in the same range as the property owner. This is an additional $14,000 to $16,000!

The lender was hoping to receive $203,600 at the foreclosure sale. This assumes someone will bid above the lender's credit bid. Remember the property is worth $210,000. What real estate investor in their right mind will bid above the lender's credit bid? No one is going to bid above the lender's credit bid. The lender will wind up winning the bid with their opening credit bid. Now the lender owns the property. What would the lender net after all costs?

Lender Payoff	$203,600
Foreclosure Costs	$4,000
Holding Costs	$6,000
Closing Costs	−$16,000
Lender's Net	$177,600

Your offer of $169,000 is now looking very attractive to the lender. The lender will not have to conduct a foreclosure sale, plus they will not have to wait six to nine months for the property to sell if no one buys the property at the foreclosure sale. They will also avoid having the holding costs and paying the closing costs. This becomes a win-win deal for you and the lender.

How do you contact the lender? No real estate lender will talk to you without their borrower's (the property owner's) permission. The borrower is the lender's client/customer. You are an outsider to whom the lender will rightly divulge no privileged or confidential information.

In the next chapter we will show you how to bypass the owner and talk directly to the lender. You must, however, make contact with the property owner before you make contact with the real estate lender. Once you have the property owner's (the borrower's) permission, you will be able to successfully contact the lender.

CHAPTER 8

How to Bypass the Owner

So now you are ready to find out how to bypass the owner. This chapter is about how to bypass the property owner and make a deal with their lender once you determine the property owner has no equity in the property and you have the property owner's permission to proceed. If the property owner has no equity in their property, there is no deal to be made with them to buy their equity.

However, you must be in contact with the property owner to make a short-sale foreclosure deal. You may not go directly to the lender without the owner's permission. When other investors determine that the property owner has no equity, this is the point at which your competition evaporates. Now is the time for you to propose making a short-sale deal with the property owner. Instead of buying the property owner's equity, you are going to buy part of the lender's equity.

Lender's Equity

At first glance, lender's equity seems like an oxymoron. In the real estate world, lender's equity sounds like the equivalent of jumbo shrimp. We typically associate equity with an ownership interest. A real estate lender loans money to a borrower to purchase real estate. The borrower is the owner of the real estate.

The lender has no ownership interest in the property. The lender has a security interest in the property. If the borrower does not pay back the borrowed money at the agreed-upon terms and conditions of the loan, the lender can take the property away from the property owner (foreclose) and sell it to recover the lender's money. The property serves as the collateral for the loan.

Let's say a property is worth $400,000. The borrower makes a 10 percent down payment of $40,000. They borrow $360,000 from a real estate lender.

Loan Amount

Value of Property	$400,000
Down Payment	−$40,000
Loan Amount	$360,000

At the moment the property is owned by the borrower, we would say that the borrower has a $40,000 equity position in the property. We would also say the lender has no equity position in the property. The lender has a promissory note for $360,000 secured by a mortgage or deed of trust, depending on whether mortgages or deeds of trust are used in the borrower's area. (See Appendix B, "Loans Chart," to determine what is preferred in your area.) Let's first talk about what typically happens when a property owner gets in a distressed situation.

Property Owner in Distress

If the property owner gets in a distressed situation, including the inability to make mortgage payments, financial trouble is sure to follow. Let's say the monthly payment for principal, interest, property taxes, and insurance is $3,200. Four months of missed payments would put the borrower in arrears almost $13,000.

In Arrears

Monthly Payment	$3,200
Missed Payments	×4
In Arrears	$12,800

Let's say the value of the property has dropped 5 percent due to a cooling of the real estate market. This is $20,000.

Dollar Drop

Value of Property	$400,000
Percentage Drop	×5%
Dollar Drop	$20,000

The property is now worth only $380,000.

New Value of Property

Value of Property	$400,000
Dollar Drop	−$20,000
New Value of Property	$380,000

The lender is owed the original $360,000 they loaned to the borrower plus the four months of payments of $12,800 that are in arrears. This is a total owed to the lender of $372,800.

Owed to Lender

Loan Amount	$360,000
In Arrears	+$12,800
Total Owed to Lender	$372,800

How much equity does the property owner currently have in the property? Remember they started out with $40,000 in equity. The new value of the property is $380,000. The total owed to the lender is $372,800. The current owner's equity is only $7,200.

Owner's Equity

New Value of Property	$380,000
Total Owed to Lender	−$372,800
Current Owner's Equity	$7,200

Wow! The property owner has gone from a $40,000 equity position to a $7,200 equity position. The property owner has lost almost $33,000 in equity! This looks like a short-sale foreclosure opportunity waiting to happen.

Lost Equity

Owner's Original Equity	$40,000
Current Owner's Equity	−$7,200
Owner's Lost Equity	$32,800

Lender as Property Owner

With foreclosure looming, the lender is about to become the property owner. There is not enough equity in the property to attract a real estate investor to make a deal with the property owner to buy the current owner's equity of $7,200.

There is also not enough equity to attract a real estate investor offering more than the lender's credit bid by the time the foreclosure sale occurs. If the lender waits to foreclose for two more months, the borrower will be six payments in arrears.

The lender will add two more months of missed payments, which is another $6,400. The lender will add an additional $3,000 to $4,000 in lender foreclosure costs. These lender foreclosure costs include attorney's fees, trustee's fees, advertising costs, and title costs. This is going to add another $10,400 to the lender's credit bid at the foreclosure sale.

Added to Credit Bid

Additional Missed Payments	$6,400
Lender Foreclosure Costs	+$4,000
Amount Added to Credit Bid	$10,400

You now have a projected lender's credit bid of $383,200.

Lender's Credit Bid

Total Owed to Lender	$372,800
Amount Added to Credit Bid	+$10,400
Projected Lender's Credit Bid	$383,200

So how is this going to look to real estate investors at the foreclosure sale?

Equity

New Value of Property	$380,000
Projected Lender's Credit Bid	−$383,200
Equity in Property	($3,200)

Yes, you are reading that correctly. The equity in the property for an investor to pick up by bidding above the lender's credit bid at the foreclosure sale is a negative $3,200. No one will bid at the foreclosure sale. The lender will become the owner of the property with their credit bid.

Before the foreclosure sale occurs, we can make a short-sale deal with the lender and buy some of the lender's equity in the property. Obviously, we want to buy the lender's equity at a substantial discount. Another way to say this is we want to buy the lender's equity for a wholesale price. So now let's talk about making a short-sale deal.

Bypassing the Owner

You approach a property owner in distress in the short-sale foreclosure arena the same way you approach a property owner in distress in the regular foreclosure arena. Once you have developed rapport with the property owner, you are in a position to make a deal.

Making a Deal with the Property Owner

You must make a deal with the property owner in order to move forward on a short-sale deal with the real estate lender. Some investors have the misguided notion that they can buy the property directly from the real estate lender once the property is in the foreclosure process. This is not possible.

The real estate lender becomes the owner of the property only at the completion of the foreclosure sale if no one outbids the lender's credit bid. In other words, the real estate lender has no authority to make a short-sale deal with you or anyone else unless, and until, the lender has the property owner's permission!

It is possible to talk to the real estate lender without the property owner's permission if you are interested in buying the mortgage paper held by the lender. Then you would become the lender and you could continue the foreclosure process. We will discuss this investment possibility in Chapter 14, "Buying the Mortgage in Foreclosure at a Short-Sale Price." That is not what we are doing here. Here we are going to give you the nine steps to a successful short-sale.

The Nine Steps to a Successful Short-Sale

It takes nine steps to complete a successful short-sale. These nine steps include finding property owners in distress, making a deal with the property owner to do a short-sale, having the property owner give you written authorization to make contact with the lender, obtaining a financial hardship letter from the property owner, assembling supporting documentation, writing a purchase contract that is signed by the property owner and you, submitting your short-sale offer to the lender, negotiating with the lender, and closing your short-sale deal.

We are going to examine these nine steps in detail. Our goal is to give you bite-sized pieces of information that you can quickly and easily digest. Some of these nine steps we have already presented. The rest of the nine steps will be presented here and in subsequent chapters. Some of the steps we will explain more completely in their own chapters.

1. Finding Property Owners in Distress
We discussed in Chapter 4, "How to Find Short-Sale Foreclosures," how to find property owners in distress. Suffice it to say that property owners in distress are everywhere. With rising interest rates, aggressive lending practices, and the cooling of

the real estate market, you will have many opportunities to assist property owners and make a good real estate deal for yourself.

2. Making a Deal with the Property Owner to Do a Short-Sale

The first step in making a deal with the property owner in distress is to determine the property owner's equity position. As we have said previously, if the property owner has an equity position in the property of at least 15 percent of the market value of the property, then you want to think about making a deal with them to buy their equity.

Let's say the property is worth $400,000. The property owner would have to have a minimum of $60,000 equity in the property for you to be interested in buying their equity. Fifteen percent of $400,000 is $60,000. Without this 15 percent equity position, you are not going to be able to make any money in the deal.

Owner's Equity

Value of Property	$400,000
Minimum Equity Percentage	×15%
Property Owner's Equity	$60,000

If the property owner has less than a 15 percent equity position in the property, you want to make a short-sale deal with them. Let's say the value of the property is $400,000. You discover the property owner's equity was originally $40,000, however. This is only a 10 percent equity position for the property owner. You are immediately thinking of making a short-sale deal with the property owner.

Owner's Equity

Value of Property	$400,000
Equity Percentage	×10%
Property Owner's Equity	$40,000

Let's review the numbers from earlier in this chapter. Let's say you buy the property owner's $40,000 equity for $10,000. You also must make up the $12,800 in back payments to the lender. Now you have $22,800 invested in the property.

Invested in Property

Amount Paid for Equity	$10,000
Back Payments to Lender	+$12,800
Amount Invested in Property	$22,800

If the value of the property has dropped to $380,000 or if you can sell it quickly for only $380,000, you will lose money. Adding the $22,800 to the $360,000 loan balance is $382,800.

Profit

Property or Sales Value	$380,000
Loan Balance	−$360,000
Property Equity	$20,000

Loss

Property Equity	$20,000
Amount Invested	−$22,800
Loss	($2,800)

3. Written Authorization to Make Contact with the Lender

Once you determine you are going to do a short-sale deal with the property owner, the next step is to obtain their written authorization to make contact with the real estate lender. As we have already mentioned, the real estate lender cannot and will not speak with you about the status of the loan, how far along the foreclosure process is, or whether they are interested in doing a short-sale deal until you present them an authorization in writing signed by the owner/borrower to release information.

This authorization form to release information can be very simple. We will present the form we use. Some lenders require the use of their own authorization form. Either you or the owner/borrower can call the lender to find out what the lender requires. What we have found works best is for you to have the owner/borrower call the lender while you are with them. If the lender requires that you use their form, ask the lender to fax their form to you immediately.

We have also found it useful to have the owner/borrower give us the last four digits of their social security number(s). This can help us gain entry to the lender sharing loan information with us in a timely manner.

AUTHORIZATION TO RELEASE INFORMATION

I/We _____, the borrower(s) of record for loan number _____, give you, _____, our lender of record, written authorization to release information regarding our loan to _____

_____.

Signed and dated this _____ day of _____, 20_____.

_____   _____

           Borrower   Borrower

4. Obtaining a Financial Hardship Letter

After you have the owner/borrower sign an authorization-to-release-information form, turn your attention to helping the owner/borrower to compose an owner hardship letter. This letter is addressed to the lender. You want to convince the lender that the owner/borrower has a real hardship situation with no hope of bringing their loan current.

The hardship letter serves two purposes. The first purpose the hardship letter serves is to present you as the lender's solution to a potential full-blown foreclosure problem. The problem for the lender is winding up owning the property after no one bids at the foreclosure sale. Your short-sale offer is the solution to the lender's problem.

The second purpose the hardship letter serves is it salvages the owner/borrower's financial situation to the extent that is now possible given its distressed condition. By agreeing to a short-sale, the owner/borrower avoids the damage of an actual foreclosure sale on their credit reports.

We are going to give you an example of an owner/borrower hardship letter. An effective hardship letter sticks to the facts and is straightforward and relatively simple. Typically, there are stringent hardship tests for an owner/borrower to satisfy in order for a lender to authorize a short-sale.

These include illness, death, divorce, job transfer, military service, disability, unemployment, incarceration, and insolvency. According to the Internal Revenue Service, "You are insolvent when, and to the extent, your liabilities exceed the fair market value of your assets."

Another word for insolvency is bankruptcy. Something to make note of is the new federal bankruptcy laws. These new bankruptcy laws went into effect in October 2005. They make it much harder to qualify for a Chapter 7 bankruptcy, wherein all your debts are wiped out. Mentioning the word *bankruptcy* in the hardship letter is still a powerful way to get the lender's attention and stimulate the lender's interest in a short-sale deal, however.

Sample Hardship Letter

July 22, 2006

To Whom It May Concern,

This is a hardship letter. I lost my job as a systems analyst. I have been unemployed for six months. I have been receiving unemployment benefits. However, my unemployment check replaces about one quarter of my previous income. I have exhausted my savings. My credit cards are maxed out. I am seriously contemplating filing for bankruptcy protection.

I can no longer afford to make the $3,200 monthly mortgage payment on my home. I am currently four months behind. I see no way to make up the almost $13,000 in back payments. I am interested in selling my property to Chantal and Bill Carey. I want to avoid a foreclosure sale that will further damage my credit. I request you work with Mr. and Mrs. Carey to negotiate a short-sale transaction.

This would be in my best interest financially. I am willing to cooperate with you as my lender to provide whatever documentation that you require in order to make this short-sale happen.

Sincerely,
Owner/Borrower

5. Assembling Supporting Documentation

There are several other documents that you will need to assemble to submit with your short-sale package. These include the owner/borrower's financial statement, payroll stubs, the owner/borrower's financial history, unemployment claims, the owner/borrower's prior two years of tax returns, six months of bank statements, credit reports, and any medical costs or a divorce decree, if applicable.

6. Writing a Purchase Contract

Now is the time to write your short-sale offer. We will devote Chapter 9, "How to Write a Short-Sale Offer," to show you the most effective way to write your short-sale offers. Keep in mind that you are making the offer to the owner/borrower first. Once you have the owner/borrower's agreement in writing to sell you their property, then you present the short-sale offer to the lender.

7. Submitting your Short-Sale Offer to the Lender

After you have made a deal with the property owner to do a short-sale, have had the property owner give you written authorization to make contact with the lender, have obtained a financial hardship letter from the property owner, have assembled supporting documentation, and have written a purchase contract that is signed by you and the property owner, you are ready to submit your short-sale offer to the lender.

Each lender has its own preferred method of processing short-sale offers. You may be able to submit your sales contract and supporting documentation to the lender by facsimile.

Some lenders will allow you to submit your offer to them by
e-mail using attachments. You may have to express ship or mail
a hard copy of the paperwork to the lender.

8. Negotiating with the Lender

Once the lender has received your short-sale offer, negotiations
are on. You may have established a rapport with the person
who works in the lender's loss mitigation department and who
has the authority to make a deal for the property you are interested in short-sale purchasing. You may think you have a deal
worked out over the phone. As with all real estate investments,
however, everything must be in writing to be valid.

We devote Chapter 12, "How to Have Your Short-Sale
Offer Accepted by the Lender," to negotiating with the lender.
By putting your short-sale offer in writing and submitting it to
the lender, you have started the true negotiating ball rolling.

9. Closing your Short-Sale Deal

The last step in a successful short-sale deal is closing the transaction. This means you give the lender the agreed-upon short-
sale loan payoff. The lender signs off on the mortgage loan,
removing the security interest the lender has against the title.
The property owner signs a deed giving you title to the property. The title insurance company insures that you are receiving
clear title. Chapter 18, "Escrow, Closing, and Title Insurance,"
will give you all the information you need to successfully close
your short-sale deal.

We now turn our attention to writing and presenting
your short-sale offer.

CHAPTER 9

How to Write a Short-Sale Offer

There are no oral agreements in real estate. Everything must be in writing. In this chapter we will show you how to write an offer that will get you a great short-sale deal and at the same time protect you from winding up in a lousy deal. We will also show you how to present your short-sale offer to the property owner in such a way that the property owner will see for themselves the advantage in accepting your offer.

Writing Your Short-Sale Offer

As we have said, there are no oral agreements in real estate. Yes, technically, you can agree to buy someone's property and they can agree to sell it to you without a written agreement. If a dispute arises between you and the property owner and you wind up in front of the judge, however, the case will be thrown out of court as soon as the judge discovers there is no written agreement.

Every state has a statute of frauds that says that in order for a real estate contract to be valid it must be in writing. If the real estate contract is not in writing, the real estate contract cannot be enforced in a court of law. If the contract cannot be enforced, the contract is not valid. If the contract is not valid, there is no contract. You get the picture.

Requirements of a Valid Contract

In addition to the requirement that a real estate contract must be in writing to be valid, a valid real estate contract must meet four other requirements. We call this the CoCa CoLa test. We are not promoting or advertising a soft drink here, but we are using CoCa CoLa as a memory aid.

Once you understand these additional four requirements for a valid real estate contract you will always use the CoCa CoLa test to make sure all the requirements are present in your real estate contracts. These requirements are consent, capacity, consideration, and lawful object.

CoCa CoLa

Consent: There must be mutual consent between the parties to the real estate contract. The parties to a real estate contract are typically the property owner and the buyer. We will find that the lender becomes a third party to a short-sale real estate contract. The parties have to agree (consent) to the wording and conditions written in the contract.

You, as the buyer, have only to sell the property owner on accepting your offer in a normal two-party real estate contract. In a short-sale transaction you, as the buyer, have to sell the property owner on accepting your offer. Then, after you have received the property owner's acceptance of your offer, you have to sell the real estate lender on accepting your short-sale offer.

Capacity: The parties to the real estate contract must have the capacity to enter into the contract. This means the parties have to be of sound mind (competent) and of legal age (18 in most places). There are some exceptions to the legal age requirement, such as being married, being married and then divorced, being in the military, or being an emancipated minor.

Consideration: Anything of value that influences a person to enter into a real estate contract is consideration.

This could be money, a deed, a service, an item of personal property, an act (including the payment of money), or a promise (including the promise to pay on a loan). If the consideration is an act or a service, that act or service must be performed after the parties enter into the real estate contract.

Usually a buyer will attach some form of earnest money to the real estate contract to satisfy the consideration requirement. This can be in the form of cash (we do not recommend cash), a check, a money order, or a promissory note.

We recommend the use of a promissory note for two reasons. First, by using a promissory note you protect your cash. Second, you do not have 10, 15, or 20 personal checks out there accompanying all those short-sale offers you are writing and presenting. You only have to turn the promissory note into cash if your offer is accepted and you are going to open an escrow.

Lawful: Real estate is lawful for people to buy and sell. For a real estate contract to be valid, the promises made between the parties must be legal to make. Also, the consideration given by the buyer must be legal to give. Now that you know the requirements of a valid contract let's look into the various types of real estate contracts.

Types of Real Estate Contracts

There are many types of real estate contracts. The purpose of any real estate contract is to communicate. We believe that the simpler the real estate contract the better the communication between the parties to the contract. You could write a real estate contract on the back of a napkin sitting in a restaurant. We have done it. But we recommend paper instead.

When we first got into the real estate business, we used a four-page real estate purchase contract in California. We heard tell from the grizzled old real estate veterans that when they first got in the business, they used a one-page real estate purchase contract!

This contract was basically a blank piece of paper. You made up your offer as you wrote it down. Talk about a simple real estate contract that would facilitate communication between the property owner and the buyer! What kind of a real estate contract should you use for your short-sale offers? We recommend you use a standard real estate purchase contract for your short-sale offers.

Real Estate Purchase Contract

A real estate purchase contract is the basic agreement between you and the property owner for purchasing their property. Many variations of real estate purchase contracts exist. You can check with local Realtors, title insurance companies, or office supply stores to obtain a copy of the type of real estate purchase contract used in your area.

For example, in Texas, the Texas Real Estate Commission (TREC) provides a standard real estate purchase contract that must be used by all real estate licensees in Texas. The TREC real estate purchase contracts can be used by nonlicensees— real estate investors—to make offers, however. You can download TREC real estate contracts from their Web site at www.trec.state.tx.us.

In Appendix C, "Contracts," we provide an example of the real estate purchase contract we use. To obtain a standard size contract (8 1/2" × 11"), see the fourth edition of our book *How to Sell Your Home Without a Broker* (John Wiley & Sons, 2004).

Remember, regardless of the type of real estate purchase contract you use, the purpose of the contract is to communicate. The more straightforwardly the real estate purchase contract states your intentions to the property owner, the easier it will be for the property owner to understand what you are trying to do. If the property owner understands what you are trying to do with your offer, then it is more likely they will be predisposed to accept your offer. In other words, the simpler your real estate purchase contract the better.

Design

Real estate purchase contracts have been designed to have standard clauses, known as the boilerplate, that are to be used for all types of transactions. The blank lines and spaces in the contract are to be used by you to customize your particular deal.

Whatever real estate purchase contract you are using, you begin by just filling in the blanks of the contract. Every blank space is either filled in, or the letters *NA* (not applicable) are written in. If you are using our contract, you fill in the city, state, and date. Then you fill in the name of the buyer (that is you!).

And/Or Assigns

Now comes the exciting part! Before going any further into the contract, we are going to stay in the "Received from" or buyer's section. We are going to add three words, and/or assigns, to this line. These are the three most powerful words you can have in a contract.

By adding *and/or assigns* to the buyer's name, we have created the opportunity for you to make money three ways rather than only one way. You can still make money the normal way by going ahead and buying the property yourself.

By adding *and/or assigns,* however, you create a second way to make money. You can bring in a money partner to fund the transaction. You and assigns, the money partner, are now buying the property.

And/or assigns also gives you a third way to make money. You can assign the contract, you or assigns, for an assignment fee to another buyer. Now the other buyer is buying the property. You are not buying the property but assigning your interest in the purchase contract to another buyer and making money without buying or owning the property.

Assigning a contract is completely straightforward and legal. An assignment of a real estate purchase contract is designed to quickly provide a real estate solution for you and the property owner. Remember our adage that the purpose of the contract is to communicate. When a property owner asks you what *and/or assigns* means, this is what you should say:

And/Or Assigns Script

"_____ (property owner's name), the AND/OR ASSIGNS clause gives both you and us the added flexibility of bringing in additional buyers or money partners to successfully close our transaction in a timely manner. Would that be all right with you?"

In our experience the property owner's answer has always been yes. Sometimes we have had to work with a property owner for a while and educate him or her on the benefits that *and/or assigns* had for them.

What do you do if the property owner's answer is no? You want to make sure the property owner understands what you are trying to do by having the ability to assign your contract. Flexibility is the name of the game in making a real estate deal work. This is especially true with a short-sale deal. If the property owner will not agree to give you the flexibility you need by having *and/or assigns* in your contract, let the property owner know that you will not proceed to present the rest of the contract.

You must stick to your guns on this point. *And/or assigns* is that important to your real estate investing success. It is much harder to come back to the negotiating table after you have already reached an agreement with the property owner. Have *and/or assigns* be part of your contract from the beginning.

A final piece regarding *and/or assigns.* Due to the new lending laws, you may find that you cannot assign your short-sale deal as readily as you could in the past. We will give you all the details in Chapter 12, "How to Have Your Short-Sale Offer Accepted by the Lender."

Financing

A short-sale offer is an all-cash offer. There are no ifs, ands, or buts when you write a short-sale offer with regard to the financing. There is no financing. Cash is king. This is why after you have negotiated a good short-sale deal you may want to bring in a money partner to put up the cash to fund the deal. All of the net cash is going to the lender. FHA will allow up to $1,000 to go to the property owner.

A lender is willing to do a short-sale based on getting their short-sale price in cash. The short-sale lender will not refinance the loan they are going to short-sale. Let's look at some numbers.

Let's say the loan balance is $152,000. You present an offer to the property owner for $102,209. At the closing, you and FHA agree to the property owner receiving $1,000. The short-sale lender will receive $101,209. The short-sale lender is taking a loss of more than $50,000. The short-sale lender will not agree to finance the $101,209.

Loan Balance	$152,000
Short-Sale Offer	$102,209
Property Owner Receives	−$1,000
Lender Receives	$101,209

After you have written your short-sale offer you must present your short-sale offer. Remember, this real estate contract is a three-party contract. The three parties are the property owner, you, and the short-sale lender. You must first present your short-sale offer to the property owner. They still own the property. Once you have the property owner accept your offer, then you present it to the lender.

Presenting Your Offer

We are going to give you a crash course in real estate offer presentation. The purpose of presenting your offer is to have the property owner accept your offer. By building rapport with the property owner, you dramatically increase the likelihood that the property owner will, eventually, accept your offer.

We have said that the purpose of the real estate contract is to communicate. You communicate best when there is a rapport between you and the property owner. The reason you want to build a rapport with the property owner is to create a relationship between you and the property owner. A relationship means a good deal for everyone. No relationship means no deal for anyone.

Building Rapport

You begin to build a rapport the moment you start an interaction with a person. We have found that being respectful toward and being interested in a property owner's situation builds rapport. You also must be an encouraging and upbeat person when you interact with a property owner to instill in the property owner the confidence that you can get a real estate transaction done.

We go into every interaction with a property owner with a win-win attitude. We want the property owner to win and we want to win. You will find as a real estate investor that getting a good deal is easy. You just have to ask. When we make an offer, we want to get a good deal, and we find that when we get a good deal, we are solving a problem for the property owner. That makes it a win-win situation for us and the property owner.

Where to Present Your Offer

We recommend presenting your offer in person. This is the most effective way to present an offer. We do not recommend presenting your offer over the phone. Presenting an offer by fax or by e-mail is less effective still.

Always present your offer at the seller's dining table. Arrange to sit at the head of the table with your back to an outside wall. You want the seller's attention focused on you and not what is going on in the rest of the house.

By presenting your offer at the dining table, you convey that this is a business situation. If you present the offer in the living room it conveys a social interaction. Ask that television and radios be turned off. Do not accept an offer of food. Accepting an offer of a beverage (nonalcoholic) is fine.

Keep the chitchat to no more than five minutes. At the appropriate time (see accompanying script), you will give the seller a copy of your offer so they can follow along with your presentation. You *are* going to make a presentation!

When to Present Your Offer

Present your offer within 72 hours of seeing a property for the first time. There are two reasons for this. The first reason has to do with you. (The second reason has to do with the property owner.) We want you to present offers within 72 hours of seeing the property for the first time so that you will present offers rather than procrastinate.

It gets very easy to find properties, look at the properties, get scared, and not write and present offers, find more properties, look at properties, get scared. Get the point? You will not make any money as a real estate investor unless you write *and* present offers. Remember, *Do it now, not later! Be Bold!*

Within 72 Hours

The reason we want you to present offers within 72 hours of seeing the property for the first time is so you will convey a sense of urgency and interest to the property owner. Property owners want to know that you are a serious buyer. Serious buyers take action in a timely manner. That is why it says on most real estate contracts, "Time is of the essence."

How to Present Your Offer

We want to give you a script to use when you are presenting offers. The script is the same no matter what kind of real estate contract you are presenting. This may seem too simple for those of you who are experienced investors. If you have something that works for you, then by all means use it.

Practice the script in the mirror at home or with your real estate investment partner before you try it for real with a property owner. After the five minutes of chitchat at the property owner's dining table, this is what you say and do.

Script

Pull out of your briefcase or folder two copies of your offer. Place them face down facing you on the table in front of you. Look at the seller and say:

"**Mr. and Mrs. Property Owner** (if you are on a first-name basis, use the property owner's first name[s]), **we are so excited to be able to present our offer to purchase your property.**" Pause for their response.

Smiling. "**Thank you for allowing us to come into your home.**" Pause. "**As you know, we are real estate investors.**" Pause. "**Our offer is designed to solve your real estate problems.**" Pause. Nodding your head up and down. "**We want to do business with you. Before we go over the offer, we just want to make sure you still want to sell your property. Do you still want to sell your property?**" Pause and wait for "Yes."

"**Are you ready to go over the offer?**" Pause and wait for a second "Yes."

Turn over the two copies of your offer, which should be facing you and be upside down or sideways to them. Do not give them their copy yet!

"**If we can solve your real estate problems, can we do business?**" Pause and wait for the third "Yes."

Now give them their copy of the offer.

Three Responses

There are three responses a property owner can have to your short-sale offer. The property owner can accept your offer, counter your offer, or reject your offer. If the property owner accepts your short-sale offer, you have a contract to take to the lender. If the property owner counters your short-sale offer, you have something to work with. If the property owner rejects your short-sale offer, you may be at a dead end. Obviously, you do not want the property owner to say no.

You cannot help the property owner solve their real estate problems without making money for yourself. You are a real estate investor, not a real estate philanthropist. Do not buy the property owner's problems. The purpose of the script is to have the property owner be receptive to your offer. If the property owner does not accept your offer, talk over the sticking points and ask the property owner for a counteroffer.

Know what you and your money partners are prepared to do before you accept a counteroffer from the property owner. We have found that we can create a win-win situation for us and the property owner by using the script. Stick with the script!

In the next chapter we will show you what to do after you have reached a meeting of the minds with the property owner. Just because the property owner has accepted your short-sale offer or you have accepted the property owner's counteroffer does not mean you have made any money. Next on the agenda is presenting your property owner's accepted short-sale offer to the real estate lender.

CHAPTER 10

Buying from the Lender before the Foreclosure Sale

In this chapter we will show you how to negotiate with the lender after you have negotiated an accepted short-sale offer with the property owner. If you are looking for the information on how to negotiate with the lender after the foreclosure sale, please see Chapter 16, "Buying from the Lender after the Foreclosure Sale."

Before we talk about negotiating with the lender, we need to give you some information on how real estate title-to-property and real estate financing-of-property interact. This is the paperwork of real estate. Once you have this information, you will better understand real estate lenders' perspectives and how best to negotiate a short-sale contract with them.

Real Estate Paperwork

Understanding the paperwork of real estate is critical to your success as a real estate investor. In this chapter we are going to talk about the paperwork involved in the owner's title and lender financing. In Chapter 18, "Escrow, Closing, and Title Insurance," we will talk about the paperwork necessary for you, as a real estate investor, to make and close deals.

There are three aspects to the title and lending paperwork. First, there is the paperwork involved on the title side.

Second, there is the paperwork involved on the financing side. Finally, there is the paperwork bridging the title side and the financing side known as the security side. Let's start with the title side.

Title Side

Using the United States as an example, on the title side there are two types of deeds used to convey the property title from one owner to the next. These two deeds are grant deeds and warranty deeds. To find out which deed is used in your area of the United States, see Appendix A, "Deeds Chart." For other countries, check with your local title conveyance official or law agent specializing in title conveyance.

Grant Deed

A *grant deed* is a deed using the word *grant* in the clause that awards ownership. This written document is used by the grantor (seller) to transfer the title of their property to the grantee (buyer). Grant deeds have two implied warranties. One is that the grantor has not previously transferred the title. The second is that the title is free from encumbrances that are not visible to the grantee. This deed also transfers title acquired after delivery of the deed from the seller to the buyer. Delivery means the seller has signed the deed and deposited the deed in escrow.

Warranty Deed

A *warranty deed* is a deed in which the grantor (usually the seller) guarantees the title to the property to be in the condition indicated in the deed. The grantor agrees to protect the grantee (usually the buyer) against all claims to the property made by anyone other than holders of recorded liens (matters of record). A warranty deed gives a warranty to the title holder.

Title Side

Grant Deed		*Warranty Deed*	
Grantor	Grantee	Grantor	Grantee
(Seller	(Buyer)	(Seller	(Buyer)
or		or	
Owner)		Owner)	

Now let's discuss the financing side.

Financing Side

The paperwork involved on the financing side is the evidence of the debt. The two types of paperwork that are used as evidence of the debt are the promissory note and the mortgage note. This paperwork is used by lenders and borrowers to create a written agreement about the terms and conditions of the real estate loan.

Promissory Note

A *promissory note* is the written contract a borrower signs promising to pay back a definite amount of money by a definite future date to a lender. A promissory note has four basic elements. These are the amount of the note, the interest rate of the note, the term of the note, and the payments, if any, on the note. A promissory note that has no payments till the due date of the note is called a straight note.

Mortgage Note

A *mortgage note* is a written contract signed by a borrower in which the borrower agrees to pay back a lender the amount of money the lender loaned the borrower. Similar to a promissory note, a mortgage note specifies the amount of the note, the interest rate of the note, the term of the note, and the payments on the note.

Financing Side

Promissory Note		*Mortgage Note*	
Borrower	Lender	Borrower	Lender
(Maker of	(Holder of	(Maker of	(Holder of
the Note)	the Note)	the Note)	the Note)

Finally let's talk about the bridge between the title side and the financing side known as the security side.

Security Side

The paperwork involved on the security side is trust deeds and mortgage contracts. They are regarded as security devices for the promissory notes and mortgage notes, respectively. Another way to say this is the trust deed and mortgage contracts are the collateral for the lender in the event a borrower defaults on the loan.

They become liens against the property title when they are officially recorded at the county recorder's office in the county where the property that is the security or collateral for the lien is located. For U.S. readers to find out which security device is used in your area please see Appendix B, "Loans Chart." Other readers please check with your local records office.

Trust Deed

A *trust deed* is a document, used as a security device for a loan on a property, by which the owner transfers bare (naked) legal title with the power of sale to a trustee. This transfer is in effect until the owner totally pays off the loan.

There are three parties to a trust deed. These three parties are the trustor, the trustee, and the beneficiary. The trustor is the owner/borrower who transfers the bare legal title with a power of sale to the trustee. The trustee is a person who holds the bare legal title to a property without being the actual owner of the property. The trustee has the power of sale for the lender's benefit. The beneficiary is the lender of money on a property used in a trust deed type of loan.

Trust Deed

| 1 Trustor | 2 Trustee |
| (Borrower) | (Power of Sale) |

3 Beneficiary
(Lender)

Mortgage Contract

A mortgage contract is a document, used as a security device for a loan on a property, by which the owner/borrower promises their property as security or collateral without giving up possession of or title to the property.

There are two parties to a mortgage contract. These two parties are the mortgagor and the mortgagee. The mortgagor is the owner/borrower who uses a mortgage contract to borrow money. The mortgagee is the lender of money on a property used in a mortgage contract loan.

Mortgage Contract

| 1 Mortgagor | 2 Mortgagee |
| (Borrower) | (Lender) |

What It All Means

Foreclosure is possible because of the paperwork of real estate. The relationship of the title paperwork, the financing paperwork, and the security paperwork gives the lender the ability to protect their interest in a property when they loan money to a borrower.

The security paperwork—trust deeds and mortgage contracts—is the bridge between the ownership, or title, side and the finance side. The promissory notes and mortgage notes create the security devices that become liens against the title to the property.

Once you understand the paperwork of real estate you will be able to negotiate on an equal footing with real estate lenders. This is especially important when you are negotiating with lenders in the short-sale arena. All this paperwork comes down to contracts. All contracts come down to what the paperwork says. When you understand what the paperwork says, then you can control what happens to property. See if this next illustration helps clarify the paperwork relationships.

The Paperwork

Title	Security Devices	Finance
Grant Deed or	Trust Deed————Promissory Note	
Warranty Deed	Trustor/Trustee	
Grantor/Grantee	Beneficiary	
(Seller)/(Buyer)	(Lender)	
	Mortgage Contract————Mortgage Note	
	Mortgagor/Mortgagee	
	(Borrower)/(Lender)	

Now that you understand the title and financing paperwork and the corresponding security devices for them, we can move on to negotiating with the lender of the owner.

Negotiating with the Lender before You Put a Deal Together

In a situation in which you find the property owner has at least a 15 percent equity position in the property and you want to buy the owner's equity, we suggest negotiating with the lender before you put any agreement together with the property owner. That way you know how the lender is going to behave. This will eliminate any nasty surprises from the lender down the road. You will need the owner's permission to speak with their lender (see Chapter 8, "How to Bypass the Owner," for an Authorization to Release Information form).

Although you may be following a quick cash strategy, you may have to hold on to a property longer than you planned. One of the most important areas to negotiate is how the lender is going to respond if you buy the owner's equity and want to take over the existing loan. Most real estate loans have a due-on-sale clause and/or a prepayment penalty.

If the lender wants to play hardball, they can begin foreclosure proceedings against you if you do not agree with what they may want to do to modify the existing loan. These modifications could include charging an assumption fee, raising the interest rate, increasing the monthly payment, or adding a prepayment penalty.

We are going to give you an overview of the due-on-sale clause. We will also show you the difference between an assumable loan and a subject-to loan. And what is a prepayment penalty, anyway?

Due-on-Sale Clause

A *due-on-sale clause* is a type of acceleration clause in a promissory note, mortgage note, trust deed, or mortgage contract that gives a lender the right to demand all sums owed to be paid immediately if the owner transfers title to the property.

The legality of the due-on-sale clause was argued all the way to the U.S. Supreme Court in the 1980s. To unify all the states under one legal interpretation, Congress passed the Garn-St. Germain lending bill in 1986. Unfortunately, the due-on-sale clause is legal and enforceable by lenders in the United States. Other readers, please check with your local law agent for the rules in your area.

Assumable Loan

An *assumable loan* is an existing promissory note or mortgage note secured by a trust deed or mortgage contract, respectively, that is kept at the same interest rate and terms as when the original borrower financed the property.

When you assume a loan, you become primarily liable for the payments and any deficiency judgment arising from a loan default. The borrower/owner becomes secondarily liable for the payments and any deficiency judgment.

Remember, a deficiency judgment is a court decision making an individual personally liable for the payoff of a remaining amount due on a loan because less than the full amount was obtained by foreclosure on the property.

Lenders typically charge an assumption fee for you to assume a loan. They also want you to qualify for the loan, as if you were originating a new loan rather than assuming an existing loan.

Subject-to Loan

A *subject-to loan* is an existing loan for which the buyer agrees to take over responsibility for payments under the same terms and conditions as existed when the original borrower financed the property. The original borrower remains primarily responsible for any deficiency judgment in the event of a loan default, however.

The name *subject-to loan* comes from the fact that the buyer takes over the existing loan subject to the same terms and conditions. The interest rate is the same. The monthly payments are the same. Everything about the loan stays the same. There is no lender approval required for you to take over a subject-to loan as there is when you assume a loan.

We say it this way: When you assume a loan, you are entering into a formal agreement with the lender. When you take over a loan subject to, there is no formal agreement with the lender. Subject-to loans do not have a due-on-sale clause in their paperwork.

Therefore, the lender cannot threaten you with calling the loan due on sale when you have made a deal with the owner to transfer title. Pre-1988 Department of Veterans Affairs (VA) guaranteed loans and pre-1986 Federal Housing Administration

(FHA) insured loans are subject-to loans. Also, many privately held owner financing loans may be subject-to loans.

Prepayment Penalty

A prepayment penalty is a fine imposed on a borrower by a lender for early payoff of a loan or any early payoff of a substantial part of the loan. To find out if there is a prepayment penalty on a loan, as with the due-on-sale clause, check the loan documents. Most prepayment penalties lapse once the loan is on the books for five years.

The amount of the prepayment penalty is usually stated as a certain number of months' interest in addition to the amount remaining on the loan as of the payoff date. Prepayment penalties can be six months' interest or more. This can be quite a substantial amount.

Let's look at an example. What is the prepayment penalty on a loan if the remaining loan balance is $200,000, the annual interest rate is 7 percent, and the prepayment penalty is 6 months' interest?

Prepayment Penalty

Loan Balance	$200,000
Interest Rate	×7%
Annual Interest	$14,000
6 Months' Interest	$7,000

A lender cannot legally enforce receiving a prepayment penalty as a result of a foreclosure sale. The problem for you as a real estate investor is that the prohibition on the lender receiving a prepayment penalty as a result of a foreclosure sale is lifted if you buy the owner's equity in preforeclosure.

Whipsaw Effect

A lender can have an owner/borrower, or in this case, you, an investor, caught between the due-on-sale clause and the prepayment penalty. As you attempt to help the owner out of a foreclosure situation, we have suggested you buy their equity. You may encounter what we call the whipsaw effect with the lender.

If you try to take over the owner's existing loan subject to and it is not a subject-to loan, the lender can call the loan all due and payable using the due-on-sale clause. If you tell the lender you are going to pay off the loan and the loan is less than five years old and stipulates a prepayment penalty, you may get stuck paying the prepayment penalty! Let's look at negotiating with the lender after you put a deal together with the owner.

Negotiating with the Lender after You Put a Deal Together

You may prefer negotiating with the lender after you have put an agreement together with the owner. Some investors find it a waste of time to negotiate with the lender before they have put an agreement together with the owner. After they have their ducks lined up with the lender, they have found when they go back to the owner, they cannot reach an agreement to buy the owner's equity.

In a short-sale situation in which the property owner has little or no equity (less than a 15 percent equity position), you will talk to the lender only after you have a signed contract with the property owner. Otherwise you will be wasting your time. The lender can agree to do a short-sale only after you have a signed real estate purchase contract from the property owner.

Talking to the Lender

The earlier in the foreclosure process the lender is contacted, the better it is for the owner/borrower. Sometimes an owner/borrower will call their lender and say, "We haven't missed a payment yet, but we are afraid we are about to." Lenders agree that they want to know about a borrower's financial distress well ahead of the borrower missing that first loan payment.

As far as the lender is concerned, this is the perfect time for the owner in distress to call them. A spokeswoman for the Federal National Mortgage Association (Fannie Mae) puts it this way: "Don't hide from your lender. If you contact your loan servicer, most of the time you will stay in your home." Fannie Mae is the largest purchaser of home mortgages in the secondary mortgage market.

After you receive an owner's permission to talk to their lender, we suggest the following approach. Call up the lender and identify yourself as a real estate investor who is working with the owner. Find out from the lender exactly where the owner is in the foreclosure process.

It has been our experience that half the time some type of loan workout plan is put together. The other half of the time, when a loan workout plan is not put together, is when you have your opportunity to make money with a short-sale.

You want to know from the lender three things. How much time will you have to do something with the property before the foreclosure sale? How much money will it cost to delay the foreclosure sale? Will the lender consider a short-sale?

Brain Trust

We want to give you a Brain Trust idea to keep in the back of your mind when you are negotiating with the lender. Ask

them if they would consider selling the promissory or mortgage note to you. Of course, you would want to buy it for a
substantial discount from the remaining balance on the note.
After all, the note may be headed to foreclosure if it is not
already in default.

If you do wind up buying the note from the lender,
you now have two options. You can work out a deal with
the owner for the equity, as before, or you can proceed with
the foreclosure as the lender. We will show you how to do the
latter in Chapter 14, "Buying the Mortgage in Foreclosure at a
Short-Sale Price."

In Chapter 12 we will show you how to have your short-
sale offer accepted by the lender. Once you find the person in
charge, your strategy is to negotiate directly with that person
and no one else. First, you need to understand the lender's
point of view.

CHAPTER 11

Understanding Short-Sales from the Lender's Point of View

In this chapter we are going to take you inside the loss mitigation departments of real estate lenders. By understanding short-sales from the lender's point of view, you will be able to communicate more effectively with the lender's short-sale decision maker.

We are going to present the 12 factors that a lender will consider before accepting a short-sale offer. The better understanding you have of these 12 factors, the more likely the lender will agree to accept your short-sale offer.

Twelve Short-Sale Lender Factors

1. Number of Lender Nonperforming Loans

A performing loan is a loan a lender has on its financial statement as an asset. The loan is considered a performing loan if the lender is receiving payments as scheduled.

A nonperforming loan is a loan that a lender has on its financial statement as a liability. The loan is considered a nonperforming loan if the lender is receiving no payments as scheduled.

Every lender must maintain an acceptable financial statement to remain in business. If a lender is carrying too high a percentage of nonperforming loans on its financial statement, the lender gets in trouble with the federal lending regulators.

As interest rates continue to go up and the real estate market cools, lenders will experience an increase in the number of nonperforming loans. This will contribute to greater opportunities for short-sale deals to be made with lenders that are accumulating nonperforming loans. A lender's acceptance of your short-sale offer lowers the number of nonperforming loans in the lender's loan portfolio.

2. Lender Financial Condition

Federal lending regulators give real estate lenders a grace period to have nonperforming loans become performing loans again before the nonperforming loans become a lender financial statement liability. This grace period is typically 180 days (six months).

Nonperforming loans are still counted as assets for the lender during the grace period. After the grace period ends, the nonperforming loans are shifted from the asset side of the lender's financial statement to the liability side of the lender's financial statement. This is a bad thing for the lender.

If a lender can do a short-sale with a nonperforming loan before the grace period ends, the nonperforming loan never moves over to the liability side of the financial statement. We recommend you bring this information to the attention of the person you are dealing with in the lender's loss mitigation department. This may help them with their superiors to get your short-sale deal accepted. After all, their job is to mitigate lender losses (liabilities). You are helping them do their job when you give them an opportunity to accept your short-sale offer!

3. Third-Party Investor's Financial Condition

You will find that four out of five short-sale opportunities involve a third-party investor who has purchased the loan from the original lender. These third-party investors operate in the secondary mortgage market. The secondary mortgage market was created in the 1930s in response to the failure of banks and thrifts during the Great Depression. People would put their money in a bank and in return receive a passbook noting their deposit. The bank would then loan the money from all the passbooks to people in the community to finance things like real estate purchases.

When the Depression hit, people panicked and went to the banks to get their money. Unfortunately, the banks were holding mortgage paper and did not have the cash on hand to give all the passbook holders their cash. That caused many, many banks to fail.

The Federal National Mortgage Association (Fannie Mae) was created to keep liquidity in the banking system. People would still put their money in the banks, and the banks would still loan that money to consumers in the primary mortgage market so they could finance their real estate purchases. The banks would receive mortgage paper from the borrowers in return for the loan proceeds.

The banks turn around and sell the mortgage paper to Fannie Mae for cash. Fannie Mae then packages millions of dollars of mortgage paper and creates a pool of securities that is backed by the mortgages. Fannie Mae then sells these mortgage-backed securities to large institutional investors to get its cash back. Then the cycle repeats.

The Primary and Secondary Mortgage Market

```
<~~~~~~~~~~~ Money          <~~~~~~~~~~ Money
Primary                    Secondary
Borrowers~~~~~Lenders~~~~~Fannie Mae~~~~~Investors
        Market                    Market
Paper ~~~~~~~~~~~~~~~>      Paper ~~~~~~~~~~~~~~~>
```

Entities like Fannie Mae and the Federal Home Loan Mortgage Corporation (Freddie Mac) are third-party investors. Both Fannie Mae and Freddie Mac have increased exposure to foreclosures and nonperforming real estate loans. Freddie Mac is a stockholder-owned corporation chartered by Congress in

1970 to keep money flowing to mortgage lenders in support of homeownership and rental housing.

Freddie Mac purchases single-family and multifamily residential mortgages and mortgage-related securities, which it finances primarily by issuing mortgage pass-through securities and debt instruments in the capital markets. As you make short-sale offers, you will wind up dealing with these third-party investors.

4. Third-Party Investor's Loss Mitigation Department

First there was the borrower and the lender. When the original lender sells its mortgage paper on the secondary mortgage market, the original lender becomes the servicing lender for the third-party investor (Fannie Mae or Freddie Mac). If there is to be a short-sale, the third-party investor's loss mitigation department will be involved.

Fannie Mae and Freddie Mac are willing to pursue a short-sale at any time prior to the actual foreclosure sale. They will do this if their acquisition of the property is the most likely situation at the foreclosure sale. Fannie Mae will proceed with the short-sale if the proceeds of the short-sale, along with the mortgage insurance settlement (if any), will make them whole or result in a loss less than the one incurred if the property is acquired at the foreclosure sale.

Freddie Mac will approve a short-sale offer that is 90 percent to 92 percent of the broker's property opinion (BPO). Once Freddie Mac has the submission package, it will take two to three weeks to get a BPO ordered and processed.

Freddie Mac Short-Sale

Let's look at a Freddie Mac short-sale. We found a property that had been on the market for six months. The owners had moved out of town. We contacted the owners and discovered the property was about to go to a foreclosure sale. The owners had written a hardship letter to their servicing lender and included the key to the property!

We received the owner's permission to contact their servicing lender. The file had been dormant for three months. No one in the loss mitigation department knew what to do with the property once they realized the owners had sent the key.

We told the contact person in the loss mitigation department we wanted to make a short-sale offer. She told us that Freddie Mac was the third-party investor on the loan. We would have to work with Freddie Mac guidelines. Plus, she told us there was mortgage insurance (MI) on the loan.

The owners initially had the property listed with a real estate broker for $249,000. The property was five years old. Unfortunately, the real estate market had cooled in the area. Instead of being valued at $84 per square foot, the owners had dropped the real estate broker and the price to $178,000, or $60 a square foot. This is where we came in.

Carpeting needed to be replaced. The kitchen countertops and floor were blue and would have to go. The entire inside and outside of the property needed to be painted. The market comparable sales were in the $65 to $70 per square foot range.

We wrote our offer for $118,000, or $40 per square foot, had it signed by the owners, and submitted our offer to the servicing lender. The servicing lender sent copies of the offer to Freddie Mac and the mortgage insurance company.

The BPO came back at $147,500, or $50 per square foot. Ninety-two percent of $147,500 was $135,700. This was the counteroffer we received from Freddie Mac.

Broker Price Opinion	$147,500
Freddie Mac Percentage	×92%
Freddie Mac Counteroffer	$135,700

We were $17,700 apart. We countered Freddie Mac's counteroffer at $124,900. Freddie Mac accepted the $124,900. We could have financed the property but paid cash instead. We wound up paying $42 per square foot.

We replaced the carpet, painted the inside and outside of the house, and left the blue kitchen alone. We had another $5,100 in the property. We then held an auction (see our book

Going Going Gone! Auctioning Your Home for Top Dollar)
and sold the property for $177,000, or $60 per square foot.
We made $47,000 on this Freddie Mac short-sale.

Auction Price	$177,000
Money Invested	−$130,000
Our Profit	$47,000

Listing Broker

We prefer dealing with for-sale-by-owners in our short-sale
investing. You need to be prepared to deal with real estate
brokers, however. They are part of the short-sale landscape.
You may come upon a short-sale opportunity after the real
estate broker is already on the scene.

Once the borrower/owner has worked with the servicing lender and Fannie Mae or Freddie Mac to determine that
he or she is eligible for a short-sale, the borrower/owner may
select a listing broker and execute a listing agreement. All parts
of the listing agreement are between the broker and the
borrower/owner and are not negotiated by the servicing
lender, Fannie Mae, or Freddie Mac.

Fannie Mae recommends that the listing broker be prepared to distribute the submission package and real estate purchase contract to all involved institutions concurrently. These
include the servicing lender, the mortgage insurance company
(where applicable), and Fannie Mae. We concur with Fannie
Mae's recommendation.

The submission of the information to all institutions at
one time will assist expediting the acceptance and approval
process. The listing agent's direct contact must always be
with the borrower and the servicing lender, however. The
listing broker should provide any assistance necessary to
the borrower/owner in the preparation of the complete submission package.

You may develop a relationship with a real estate broker
who specializes in short-sales with third-party investors. This
can save you a lot of time and money. The broker can lead you
to short-sale opportunities and can put together the short-sale
submission package.

For Sale by Owner

If you are working with a property owner who is a for-sale-by-owner then there is no listing broker involved. Remember, the initial offer on the property must be made to the borrower, who is the owner of the property and must negotiate as such.

Once you have an accepted contract, you then contact the servicing lender and present your real estate purchase contract signed by the property owner, in copy form, to the servicing lender, Fannie Mae or Freddie Mac, and the mortgage insurer (if applicable) concurrently.

5. Servicing Lenders

Be prepared to deal with a servicing lender who is collecting the scheduled payments for a third-party investor like Fannie Mae or Freddie Mac. You will have to go through the servicing lender to deal with the third-party investor. The servicing lender is not the final decision maker for your short-sale deal.

All contact must be made with the servicing lender, however. Fannie Mae's decision and any loss mitigation will be done through the servicing lender contact person only. If the short-sale submission is distributed in its complete form to all parties concurrently, you can expect a response within two to three weeks. Please allow for this amount of time in your real estate contracts.

When Fannie Mae has received a real estate purchase contract for a short-sale, they will provide in writing to the servicing lender their approval and authorization for a short payoff. It should be pointed out that Fannie Mae does not actively negotiate or sign any of the purchase contracts. Fannie Mae can only agree to the amount of the loss it will approve.

6. Borrower's Finances

There are additional items that will be requested by the lender from the property owner in addition to the real estate purchase contract. Coordinating the distribution of these items will help expedite the decision-making process.

Submission Package

The submission package should include the borrower's letter of hardship, current financial statement, current pay stub, and the prior year's tax return. If the borrower is self-employed, they will need a copy of a year-to-date profit and loss statement, all schedules to the tax return, and a copy of any partnership or corporate tax returns, if applicable.

Fannie Mae will request copies of the current payoff statement, collection records, payment history, mortgage insurance information, and the origination documents from the servicing lender. This also includes the original mortgage application package and appraisal.

7. *Mortgage Insurance*

After Fannie Mae or Freddie Mac receives the complete submission package, they will work with the servicing lender. They will also coordinate with the mortgage insurance company to determine any preclaim settlement agreement and negotiate the mitigation of their loss.

Once all the information has been received, Fannie Mae or Freddie Mac will coordinate with all parties through the servicing lender. Depending on their financial statement, there may be a requirement for the borrower to participate in the reduction of any potential loss to Fannie Mae or Freddie Mac by signing a promissory note.

8. *As-Is Value of the Property*

The as-is value of the property is determined using the existing condition of the property with no repairs or deferred maintenance being done. Two broker price opinions (BPOs) are ordered. These may be compared with the original appraisal to see the deterioration, if any, of the value of the property.

Broker price opinions are used in lieu of paying for a formal appraisal. The lender relies on these broker price opinions as an indication of the comparative market value of the property in the current real estate market.

The servicing lender is responsible for ordering the two broker price opinions. They must be ordered from two separate sources that are not involved in the listing or sale of the property.

9. Costs to Repair Property for Resale

Real estate purchase contracts that require repairs or maintenance to the property that the property owner cannot financially afford to complete must be explained. Two written bids must be submitted with the agreement to Fannie Mae for their inclusion in the short-sale. These repairs may be presented to and negotiated with the servicing lender and the homeowner's insurance company.

10. Repaired Value

The repaired value gives the lender the ability to estimate if it would be worth it for the lender to foreclose, repair the property, and put in on the market. A lender would consider doing this if it felt it would be able to recoup the defaulted mortgage, the back payments, the foreclosure costs, and the repair costs from the proceeds of a sale.

11. Cost of Securing and Maintaining Property

A lender will estimate the cost of securing and maintaining a property that it may take back in a foreclosure sale. Securing a property includes protecting it from vandalism, repairing broken doors and windows, and turning on the water and utilities.

Maintaining a property includes removing rubbish and debris, mowing the lawn, taking care of the landscaping, watering, and keeping a pool or spa in good operating order. Securing and maintaining a property is necessary to be able to market the property effectively and receive the highest price.

12. Cost of Holding and Selling Property

A lender will estimate the cost of holding and selling a property that it takes back in a foreclosure sale. Holding the property includes making necessary repairs, painting, and replacing damaged or broken built-in appliances, water heaters, heating and air conditioning units, and carpeting and floor coverings.

Selling the property involves signing a listing agreement with a real estate broker, paying a real estate commission, and waiting four to six months or longer to find a buyer and close escrow. In addition to water and utility costs, the lender will also be responsible for property taxes and hazard insurance through the selling period.

Understanding the 12 short-sale lender factors increases the likelihood that your short-sale offer will communicate to the lender. As we have emphasized, the purpose of any real estate contract is to communicate. By understanding short-sales from the lender's point of view, your short-sale offer presents solutions to the lender's problems.

In the next chapter we will show you how to have your short-sale offer accepted by the lender. We will present our 18-point checklist for short-sale investing. By following the checklist, you will provide everything the lender needs to approve your short-sale offer.

CHAPTER 12

How to Have
Your Short-Sale Offer
Accepted by the Lender

Once you understand short-sales from the lender's point of view, you are in a position to package your short-sale offer. We recommend using a checklist to make sure you include everything necessary to have your short-sale offer accepted by the lender.

We will present our short-sale offer checklist in a narrative fashion. We will expand on some of the points of the checklist that are introduced here for the first time. You may find that you want to add or subtract items to your short-sale checklist according to what works best for you as you develop your own way of processing your short-sale offers.

The point of the short-sale checklist is to facilitate your assembling the paperwork and documents necessary to present the best possible short-sale submission package to the lender. The more complete your submission package, the easier it will be for the lender to accept your short-sale offer.

We will use an actual short-sale example to make the short-sale checklist come alive for you. We have mentioned these numbers from our example in the Preface and Chapter 7, "No Equity? No Problem!"

Short-Sale Example

We found an owner that was three months behind on the $1,200 monthly mortgage payment. The amount outstanding on the loan was $200,000. The lender was about to foreclose. The lender would like to receive the $200,000 loan balance plus $3,600 for the three back payments.

Loan Balance	$200,000
Back Payments	+$3,600
Lender's Desired Payoff	$203,600

The property was worth $210,000. The owner had little or no equity in the property.

Property Value	$210,000
Lender's Desired Payoff	−$203,600
Owner's Equity	$6,400

Assuming the owner could sell the property for $210,000, the closing costs would be in the $14,000 to $16,000 range (real estate commissions, escrow fees, attorneys' fees, and title insurance). The owner would have to put almost $10,000 into the deal! The owner did not have the $3,600 to make up their back payments let alone the $10,000 needed to sell the property.

Owner's Equity	$6,400
Closing Costs	−$16,000
Additional Owner Money	$9,600

As real estate investors, it appeared that there was no way for us to make money in this situation either. Our competition definitely thought there was no way to make money on this deal. Actually, we had no competition because 90 percent to 95 percent of our competition had already walked away.

We made a deal with the owner to buy the property for $169,000. We explained to the owner that we would have to have the lender agree to do a short-sale. This would be the only way we could buy the owner's property. If the lender would not agree to do a short-sale there would be no deal.

There were several benefits to the owner if he agreed to accept our short-sale offer. The owner would not have to make up the $3,200 in back payments. He would not have to put the additional $9,600 into selling the property. The owner would be out from under the impending lender foreclosure. He would not have to pay off the remaining loan balance. There would be no foreclosure sale against the owner's credit rating.

We had the owner sign our real estate purchase contract. We had the owner sign an authorization to release information from the lender. We then helped him write a hardship letter. Using the short-sale checklist, we then went about assembling the remaining information and documentation for our short-sale submission's package.

This included an owner financial statement, an owner financial history, owner payroll stubs, and copies of the previous two years of owner tax returns. We also made copies of the last six months of the owner's bank statements, a copy of his unemployment award letter, and copies of unpaid medical bills.

We then assembled our market comparable properties (comps) showing the lowest sales in the area that were similar to the property we were interested in buying, filled out a HUD 1 closing statement, put together two repair cost estimates, and took pictures of the property. These pictures showed the property in its worst possible light.

So now let's take a look at the short-sale checklist. This checklist makes it easy to remember what to include in your short-sale submission package.

Short-Sale Checklist

1. Your short-sale proposal letter.
2. Signed borrower authorization to release information.
3. Borrower's signed short-sale payoff application.
4. Owner hardship letter.

5. Owner financial statement.
6. Owner financial history.
7. Owner payroll stubs.
8. Two years of owner tax returns.
9. Six months of owner bank statements.
10. Owner credit reports.
11. Unemployment benefits or status.
12. Medical bills.
13. Divorce decree.
14. Signed owner/borrower short-sale purchase contract.
15. Market comparables.
16. HUD 1 or customary closing net sheet for your country.
17. Repair cost estimates.
18. As-is pictures.

Let's get into the short-sale checklist in more detail.

1. Your Short-Sale Proposal Letter

We recommend you write a short-sale proposal letter to accompany your short-sale offer. This letter is a one-page synopsis of your short-sale purchase contract.

This proposal letter should be placed at the top of the submissions package and should be the first thing the lender sees. Here is a sample short-sale proposal letter.

July 22, 2006

Short-Sale Proposal for 711 Lucky Street Oceanside, USA

To: The Loss Mitigation Department of ABC Lending Company.

Attention: Samantha Sanchez, Loss Mitigation Specialist

From: Chantal and Bill Carey 817-555-2614

Regarding: 711 Lucky Street, Oceanside, USA

Dear Ms. Sanchez,

We have a signed real estate purchase contract with your borrower Nicholas E. Macinernie, the owner of 711 Lucky Street, Oceanside, USA. Mr. Macinernie has agreed to sell us his property for a purchase price of $169,000.

Your current loan balance for loan 78934564321 is $200,000. Mr. Macinernie is three payments behind in the amount of $3,600. He has lost his job as a systems analyst and is receiving unemployment.

We have provided comparable sales of properties in the area. We feel that after you do an analysis of the numbers, you will realize that it is in your best interest to accept our all-cash offer. We look forward to doing business with you.

Sincerely,
Chantal and Bill Carey

2. Signed Borrower Authorization to Release Information

You must have a signed borrower authorization to release information before the borrower/owner's lender can legally talk to you. This authorization to release information can be very simple. We gave you a blank form in Chapter 8, "How to Bypass the Owner." Here is the authorization to release information filled out for this transaction.

Authorization to Release Information

I/We _____ Nicholas E. Macinernie _____, the borrower(s) of record for loan number 78934564321, give you, __ABC Lending Company,__ our lender of record, written authorization to release information regarding our loan to _____ Chantal or Bill Carey_____ .

Signed and dated this <u>22nd</u> day of <u>   July, 2006   </u>.

<u>   Nicholas E. Macinernie   </u>   <u>   </u>

        Borrower   Borrower

3. Borrower's Signed Short-Sale Payoff Application

The short-sale payoff application is provided by the lender. You may have obtained this in advance of your putting together your short-sale submission package. If that is the case, you will have the borrower/owner fill out and sign the short-sale payoff application and submit it as part of your package.

Some lenders will provide this to the borrower/owner only after receiving the submission package. If this is the case, we recommend you help the borrower/owner fill it out. Make sure he signs it. Then take the application and fax, e-mail, or mail a copy to the lender.

Do not wait for the borrower/owner to do anything. You must be proactive or your short-sale deal will die for lack of timely follow-through. Remember, the borrower/owner is already in trouble and may not be operating at a normal emotional mental capacity.

4. Owner Hardship Letter

Hardship Letter

July 22, 2006

To Whom It May Concern:

This is a hardship letter. I lost my job as a systems analyst. I have been unemployed for six months. I have been receiving unemployment benefits. However, my unemployment check replaces about one quarter of my previous income. I have exhausted my savings.

My credit cards are maxed out. I am in the process of filing for a divorce.

I can no longer afford to make the $1,200 monthly mortgage payment on my home. I am currently three months behind. I see no way to make up the $3,600 in back payments. I am seriously contemplating filing for bankruptcy protection.

I have agreed to sell my property to Chantal and Bill Carey for $169,000. I want to avoid a foreclosure sale that will further damage my credit. I request you work with Mr. and Mrs. Carey to negotiate a short-sale transaction.

This would be in my best interest financially. I am willing to cooperate with you as my lender to provide whatever documentation that you require in order to make this short-sale happen.

Sincerely,
Nicholas E. Macinernie
Borrower/Owner

5. Owner Financial Statement

An owner financial statement can be very simply constructed. An owner financial statement lists all the owner's assets, such as real estate, stocks, bonds, mutual funds, collectibles, and bank accounts. Then you list all the owner's liabilities, such as the current real estate loan that is in arrears, personal loans, credit card debt, law suits, judgments, and IRS liens.

In our experience we have found that the owner's liabilities usually exceed his assets. Sometimes this can be by a substantial amount. When your liabilities exceed your assets you are said to have a negative net worth.

Mr. Macinernie's financial statement certainly fell into this category.

Owner Financial Statement

Assets		Liabilities
$210,000	Real Estate Owned	
	Real Estate Loan	$200,000
	Back Monthly Payments	$3,600
	Credit Card Debt	$19,700
$15,000	Car	
	Car Loan	$17,000
	Medical Bills	$4,300
$225,000		$244,600

Some lenders want you to include all the monthly expenses in addition to the assets and liabilities. This would include house payments, car payments, utility bills, credit card bills, medical bills, insurance costs, tuition expenses, child support, food, clothing—anything that the borrower is obligated to pay monthly.

6. Owner Financial History

Mr. Macinernie's financial history was not good. He had been experiencing a series of financial setbacks for the past 18 months. He had lost his job. His unemployment benefits had run out. He was borrowing from one credit card to make the monthly payment on another credit card. He was three months behind on his mortgage payments. He was contemplating bankruptcy.

If you encounter an owner who is in bankruptcy, you have to alter your short-sale plans. The bankruptcy court has the final say in whether your short-sale will go through. We will cover what to do if you encounter an owner bankruptcy in Chapter 17, "Bankruptcy and Other Problems."

7. Owner Payroll Stubs

For this deal, there were no pay stubs to provide. The borrower/owner was unemployed. If Mr. Macinernie was employed, providing the pay stubs as part of the submission package would allow the lender to see if the monthly take-home pay would cover the loan payments plus all the other monthly expenses.

8. Two Years of Owner Tax Returns

The lender will request the last one or two years of the borrower/owner's federal income tax returns. The lender is trying to get a complete picture of the borrower/owner's financial situation. Is the income going up? Is the income going down? Will Mr. Macinernie be able to make loan payments if the lender agrees to a repayment program? Does Mr. Macinernie want to continue making payments? Mr. Macinernie made it very clear to us that he was not interested in continuing to make any more loan payments. He wanted out, period.

9. Six Months of Owner Bank Statements

The six months of bank statements is again so the lender can determine if the borrower/owner is capable of making loan payments. Mr. Macinernie's bank statements provided us with more evidence that the lender should do the short-sale deal with us. In other words, the bank statements showed he had no money.

10. Owner Credit Reports

Owner credit reports will be ordered by the lender. Sometimes the owner has a copy of his credit report. The lender will want to order its own credit report because it is the most current, however.

Mr. Macinernie's credit reports reflected his financial condition. All the credit cards were at their credit limit. Some of the accounts were 30, 60, and 90 days past due.

11. Unemployment Benefits or Status

A borrower/owner receiving unemployment benefits or being unemployed are positive indicators for your short-sale going through. Lenders are under political pressure to extend every effort to borrowers for some type of loan workout.

When it becomes obvious that the borrower has no financial wherewithal, however, the lender is off the proverbial hook. Mr. Macinernie's unemployment status was a major contributing factor in the lender agreeing to do a short-sale.

12. Medical Bills

Unfortunately, a medical need or condition with the attendant medical bills can be the reason for a borrower/owner getting into financial difficulty. If you encounter a property owner in this situation, a short-sale may be the best solution for them to get out from under a now too large mortgage payment.

Medical hardships are easy for a lender to understand. Lenders will agree to a short-sale in just about every medical hardship situation. In fact, we have never heard of a lender not agreeing to a short-sale if the borrower/owner was in a medical hardship and requested the lender to participate with an investor in a short-sale offer.

13. Divorce Decree

The number one reason people get into financial difficulty is a divorce situation. Instead of one monthly house payment, there now may be two monthly house payments. The likelihood of the lender approving a short-sale goes up dramatically when the borrowers are in a divorce situation.

14. Signed Owner/Borrower Short-Sale Purchase Contract

This one is obvious. You have to have the borrower/owner's signature on a short-sale purchase contract before you can ask the lender to agree to a short-sale. The borrower/owner is still the owner of the property. The lender cannot sell you the property. The lender does not own the property.

15. Market Comparables

The lender will order one or two broker price opinions after they receive your short-sale submission package. We have found that it will only help your cause if you provide your own market comparables. Of course, you will provide only the lowest comparables for the area of the property for which you are making your short-sale offer.

We want to make note here of an interesting phenomenon. We are finding that most of the short-sales we are doing are with properties that are less than five years old. Unlike the stereotypical run-down or dilapidated foreclosure properties, the short-sale properties we are buying are in good to excellent shape.

This means that it is relatively simple to determine the value of the property. It also means that there is agreement between us and the lender as to the market value of the property. Because we are real estate investors, the lender knows that we are interested in getting a good deal. We will only pay a wholesale price.

16. HUD 1 or Customary Closing Net Sheet for Your Country

The Department of Housing and Urban Development (HUD) has created a standardized closing statement that is used throughout the United States. This is a net sheet that lists all the credits and debits for a buyer or seller involved in a real estate transaction.

By including a net sheet in your submission package, you give the lender the bottom-line dollars in their pocket at the closing of the transaction. This is the number the person in the loss mitigation department needs to know before she can approve your short-sale offer.

You may have asked the lender to pay for things like title insurance, half the escrow fee, attorney fees, termite inspections, and repairs. All these will reduce the net cash the lender will receive.

17. Repair Cost Estimates

As we have said previously, we are buying short-sale properties that are relatively new. Therefore, we have found that we have minor repairs to make to the property in most cases.

If you are faced with a major repair, however, we recommend you ask the lender to pay for it in your short-sale offer. After all, the lender is going to have to pay for repairs if they foreclose and wind up taking the property back as a real estate owned (REO).

18. As-Is Pictures

The expression *a picture is worth a thousand words* is even truer with your short-sale package. If you are buying a property that is dilapidated or in need of repairs, by all means take pictures of the unsightly areas.

You are not trying to downgrade or devalue the property. You are trying to make the lender aware of the true condition of the property. Obviously, any money you have to spend to return the property to a good and sellable or rentable condition must be factored into your short-sale offer.

We have completed our short-sale checklist. Now we can negotiate with the lender from a position of providing everything the lender needs so they can say yes to our short-sale offer. We have made it in the best interest of the lender to accept our offer.

Negotiating with the Lender

Why did the lender accept our $169,000 short-sale offer? Because it was in the lender's best interest to do so! Remember the scenario from the lender's point of view. It is like we said before. If the lender goes through the foreclosure process and no one bids at the foreclosure sale because it looks like there is no equity in the property, the lender will still have all the foreclosure costs. These costs include posting a notice of foreclosure and advertising the foreclosure sale.

The lender will have to pay attorney's fees and trustee's fees and the foreclosure sale expenses. The lender will also have to pay for title insurance. The list goes on. The total could easily be $3,000 to $4,000.

And remember, after the lender takes back the property, they will have additional expenses. The lender will have to pay for repairs and fix-up costs, ongoing maintenance, hazard insurance, property taxes, and human resources costs. Let's call these costs holding costs. Again, the list goes on. This could easily amount to another $5,000 to $6,000.

Of course, and finally, the lender will have to put the property on the market for sale. The lender will have the closing costs and real estate commissions to pay in the same range as the seller. This is an additional $14,000 to $16,000!

The lender was hoping to receive $203,600. Assume they received this amount from the sale of the property. What would the lender net after all costs?

Lender's Net

Lender Payoff	$203,600
Foreclosure Costs	$4,000
Holding Costs	$6,000
Closing Costs	$16,000
Lender's Net	$177,600

Our offer of $169,000 is now very attractive to the lender. The lender will not have to conduct a foreclosure sale. Plus, they will not have to wait six to nine months for the property to sell if no one buys the property at the foreclosure sale. They will also avoid having the holding costs and paying the closing costs. This became a win-win-win deal for Mr. Macinernie, the lender, and us.

Our Equity

Property Value	$210,000
Negotiated Lender Payoff	$169,000
Our Equity	$41,000

In the next chapter we will show you how to make a short-sale deal when the Federal Housing Administration (FHA) is insuring the loan, the Department of Veterans Affairs (VA) is guaranteeing the loan, or a private mortgage insurance company (PMI) is insuring the loan. This just adds one more player that is involved in the short-sale transaction.

CHAPTER 13

FHA, VA, and Private Mortgage Insurance Short-Sales

In this chapter we will give you information about Federal Housing Administration (FHA), Department of Veterans Affairs (VA), and private mortgage insurance (PMI) short-sales. You may encounter one of these entities insuring or guaranteeing the loan for the lender to whom you are presenting your short-sale offer. Remember, the number one goal for the FHA, the VA, and private mortgage insurance is to do a loan-work-out plan with the borrower.

Foreclosure is their last resort. Once the FHA or the VA forecloses, then the government is in the real estate business. Just remember that both the FHA and the VA are government bureaucracies for which rules can change midstream. Be sure to verify what the rules are at the time you realize the FHA or the VA is involved in your short-sale transaction.

For example, as we were writing the manuscript for this book, hurricanes Katrina and Rita roared through Texas and the Gulf Coast. The head of the Department of Housing and Urban Development (HUD) pulled all FHA foreclosed property off the investor market and made it available to the displaced and homeless hurricane evacuees who arrived in Texas.

The best way to stay on top of what is happening at the FHA or the VA is to develop a relationship with someone on the inside of these organizations. That relationship can be worth its weight in gold. Just be prepared to be patient if you decide to participate with FHA or VA foreclosures. Let's start our discussion with the FHA.

FHA

The FHA is the mortgage insurance branch of the Department of Housing and Urban Development (HUD). Most people in the real estate arena talk about FHA loans rather than HUD loans. Technically, the FHA does not make mortgage loans. They provide mortgage insurance to real estate lenders who comply with FHA mortgage insurance loan requirements.

These loans are made at way above the lender-preferred 80 percent loan-to-value ratio. Some FHA loan programs require as little as a 3 percent down payment on the part of the borrower. The lender is making as much as a 97 percent loan-to-value ratio loan. Talk about the lender wanting some mortgage insurance protection! Essentially, the FHA is the government version of private mortgage insurance (PMI). Let's look at some numbers.

FHA Insured Loan

Purchase Price	$100,000
Down Payment	−$3,000
Mortgage Amount	$97,000

FHA Borrower Counseling

Because of the amount of exposure the FHA has when they insure real estate loans, they have developed an extensive program to counsel borrowers who are on the verge of defaulting. We are going to present some of this FHA counseling information here.

We have two purposes in mind. The first is for you to understand how the FHA thinks and operates: The FHA wants to prevent a foreclosure from occurring. The second purpose is we want you to see how the FHA presents their version of foreclosure options. You may glean some valuable information for your own foreclosure options presentation if you are dealing with an FHA owner or not. We will present this in a question-and-answer format.

FHA Question-and-Answer Format

Q. What happens when I miss my mortgage payments?

Foreclosure may occur. This is the legal means that your lender can use to repossess (take over) your home. When this happens, you must move out of your house. If your property is worth less than the total amount you owe on your mortgage loan, a deficiency judgment could be pursued. If that happens, you may not only lose your home, you may also owe HUD an additional amount.

Q. What should I do?

1. Do not ignore the letters from your lender. If you are having problems making your payments, call or write to your lender's loss mitigation department without delay. Explain your situation. Be prepared to provide them with financial information, such as your monthly income and expenses. Without this information, they may not be able to help.
2. Stay in your home for now. You may not qualify for assistance if you abandon your property.
3. Contact a HUD-approved housing counseling agency. These agencies are valuable resources. They frequently have information about services and programs offered by government agencies as well as private and community organizations that can help you. These services are usually free of charge.

Q. What are my alternatives?

You may be considered for the following:

Special forbearance: Your lender may be able to arrange a repayment plan based on your financial situation and may even provide for a temporary reduction or suspension of your payments. You may qualify for this if you have recently experienced a reduction in income or an increase in living expenses. You must furnish information to your lender to show that you would be able to meet the requirements of the new payment plan.

Mortgage modification: You may be able to refinance the debt and/or extend the term of your mortgage loan. This may help you catch up by reducing the monthly payments to a more affordable level. You may qualify if you have recovered from a financial problem and can afford the new payment amount.

Partial claim: Your lender may be able to work with you to obtain a one-time payment from the FHA insurance fund to bring your mortgage current. You may qualify if:

1. Your loan is at least 4 months delinquent but no more than 12 months delinquent.
2. You are able to begin making full mortgage payments.

When your lender files a partial claim, HUD will pay your lender the amount necessary to bring your mortgage current. You must execute a promissory note, and a lien will be placed on your property until the promissory note is paid in full. The promissory note is interest-free and is due when you pay off the first mortgage or when you sell the property.

Preforeclosure sale: This will allow you to avoid foreclosure by selling your property for an amount less than the amount necessary to pay off your mortgage loan. You may qualify if:

1. The loan is at least three months delinquent.
2. You are able to sell your house within three to five months.
3. A new appraisal (that your lender will obtain) shows that the value of your home meets HUD program guidelines.

Deed in lieu of foreclosure. As a last resort, you may be able to voluntarily give back your property to the lender. This will not save your house, but it is not as damaging to your credit rating as a foreclosure. You can qualify if:

1. You are in default and do not qualify for any of the other options.
2. Your attempts at selling the house before foreclosure were unsuccessful.
3. You do not have another FHA mortgage in default.

Q. Should I be aware of anything else?

Yes. Beware of scams! Solutions that sound too simple or too good to be true usually are. If you are selling your home without professional guidance, beware of buyers who try to rush you through the process. Unfortunately, there are people who may try to take advantage of your financial difficulty. Be especially alert to the following:

> **Equity skimming:** In this type of scam, a buyer approaches you, offering to get you out of financial trouble by promising to pay off your mortgage or give you a sum of money when the property is sold. The buyer may suggest that you move out quickly and deed the property to them. The buyer collects rent for a time, does not make any mortgage payments, and allows the lender to foreclose. Remember, signing over your deed to someone else does not necessarily relieve you of your obligation on your loan.
>
> **Phony counseling agencies:** Some groups calling themselves counseling agencies may approach you and offer to perform certain services for a fee. These could well be services you could do for yourself for free, such as negotiating a new payment plan with your lender, or pursuing a preforeclosure sale.

Q. Are there any precautions I can take?

Here are several precautions that should help you avoid being taken by a scam artist.

1. Do not sign any papers you do not fully understand.
2. Make sure you get all promises in writing.

3. Beware of any contract of sale of loan assumption in which you are not formally released from liability for your mortgage debt.
4. Check with a lawyer or your mortgage company before entering into any deal involving your home.
5. If you are selling the house yourself to avoid foreclosure, use *How to Sell Your Home Without a Broker* by Bill and Chantal Carey. (We are kidding. We are just seeing if you are really paying attention, although it would be a smart thing to do.) Check to see if there are any complaints against the prospective buyer. You can contact your state's attorney general, the state real estate commission, or the local district attorney's consumer fraud unit for this type of information.

Short-Sale

Did you pay attention to the preforeclosure sale section? It screams short-sale. The FHA says you qualify for a short-sale as the borrower/owner if you are at least three months behind in your mortgage payments, you are able to sell the house within three to five months, and your lender pays for an appraisal that shows the value of your home meets HUD guidelines.

There are several other HUD guidelines that must be met by the borrower/owner in order for the FHA to approve a short-sale. There must be a legitimate borrower hardship. The borrower must receive financial counseling through a HUD-approved entity. The most important HUD guideline is that the FHA will approve a short-sale for 82 percent of the appraised value.

Let's look at an example. We found a property that was three years old. It was in very good shape. The owners had bought the property with a 3 percent down payment and borrowed 97 percent of the purchase price from an FHA approved lender.

They paid $157,000 for the property. They made a $4,700 down payment. They borrowed $152,300. Their monthly payment was $1,400 and included principal, interest, property

taxes, mortgage, and hazard insurance. When one of the owners lost his job, they were in a financial hardship situation.

Amount Borrowed	$152,300
Down Payment	$4,700
Purchase Price	$157,000

Although the property was in a good neighborhood, the
boom in new construction had depressed the resale market.
After three years, the property was on the tax rolls at a value
of $141,600. The property was approximately 1,900 square
feet. The market comparables in the area showed that property was selling for only $64 per square foot. This meant that
the market value of the property was $121,600.

Square Feet	1,900
Price per Square Foot	×$64
Market Value	$121,600

Now here is the fun part. The FHA agreed to a short-sale
for 82 percent of the market value. We were able to buy the
property for $99,700.

Market Value	$121,600
FHA Short-Sale Percentage	×82%
Our Purchase Price	$99,700

Now let's discuss the VA.

VA

The VA can actually loan mortgage money to military person-
nel. This happens in very rural areas where a mortgage lender
may not exist. The VA predominantly acts as a guarantor of
mortgage loans for veterans purchasing homes. They act as
government mortgage insurance for real estate lenders.

The veteran can buy a home with no money down and
obtain a mortgage for 100 percent of the purchase price. Talk
about the risk to the lender!

VA Guaranteed Loan

Purchase Price	$100,000
Down Payment	−0
Mortgage Amount	$100,000

The Department of Veterans Affairs acquires properties as a result of foreclosures on VA guaranteed loans. The VA has currently awarded a contract to Ocwen Federal Bank FSB in Orlando, Florida, to manage, market, and sell these properties. At this time all VA real estate owned (REO) properties have been removed from the market and are accessible only through Ocwen Bank.

Buying VA REOs

Ocwen Federal Bank began listing VA REO properties in early 2004. The properties are listed by local listing agents through the local Multiple Listing Service (MLS). A list of properties for sale may also be obtained from Ocwen's Web site at www. ocwen.com.

If you are interested in buying one of the VA REO properties once it is listed for sale by Ocwen Federal Bank FSB, you should contact a local real estate broker to see the property and make an offer to purchase that property through that real estate broker. No longer will the VA Office of Jurisdiction manage these properties.

Our Experience

Our experience buying VA REOs, or VA repos as we call them, has been positive. At the foreclosure sale, the VA tries to get the highest amount possible for these properties. Because of the 100 percent financing, however, very often the VA cannot get anyone to outbid their credit bid at the foreclosure sale.

Let's say the VA guarantees a $100,000 loan. Two years go by, and the owner gets into financial trouble. The VA provides counseling but winds up foreclosing. The property is worth $105,000. The owner is six months and $5,000 behind in payments. The VA bids $105,000 at the foreclosure. No one is going to bid because the property value and the bid are the same amount.

VA Foreclosure

Property Value	$105,000
Credit Bid	$105,000
Profit Potential	0

Once the VA has the title to the property, they are going to make deals. Remember, they have guaranteed repayment of the loan to the actual lender. The VA is out $105,000. Any deficit between what they paid the lender and what they eventually sell the property for as a repo will be charged to the veteran borrower.

We bought this property for $77,850. We flipped this property to another real estate investor for $84,000. We made $6,150. The VA went after the borrower for a $27,150 deficiency. Rather than going to court to get a judgment against the veteran, the VA will withhold benefits if they are not paid back.

VA Repo

Flip Price	$84,000
VA Price	$77,850
Profit	$6,150

VA Short-Sales

The VA will participate in short-sales. They are called Department of Veterans Affairs compromise sales. We think that the VA will develop new guidelines over the next 12 to 18 months. As with any government program, we recommend you find out what the current guidelines are before you get too far down the road with your short-sale deal. The VA will do a short-sale for 20 percent less than the broker's price opinion.

Let's see what would happen if we did a VA compromise sale with the property we bought from the VA as a repo. We will use $95,000 as the broker's price opinion value of the property. Multiplying this by the 20 percent short-sale percentage gives us a short-sale discount of $19,000.

VA Compromise Sale

Broker's Price Opinion	$95,000
Short-Sale Percentage	×20%
Short-Sale Price Discount	$19,000

To determine the VA acceptable short-sale price, we subtract the $19,000 discount from the $95,000 broker price opinion. The VA will sell the property for $76,000.

VA Compromise Sale

Broker's Price Opinion	$95,000
Short-Sale Price Discount	−$19,000
VA Short-Sale Price	$76,000

We want you to notice that the repo price of $77,850 and the short-sale price of $76,000 are very close. This means that the VA will net approximately the same amount with a short-sale.

This becomes important in the future for two reasons. In our repo example we did not factor in how long the VA held the property before we bought it. Add three to six months of holding costs for the VA, and the VA repo bottom line would be less than the VA short-sale bottom line.

Also, as the VA encounters more borrower defaults, the VA will want to dispose of problem properties before the foreclosure sale. Otherwise, the VA is going to be overwhelmed in its REO department. Finally, we will talk about PMI-related short-sales

PMI

Private mortgage insurance (PMI) companies are heavily committed in today's real estate market. They are insuring lenders for the risk associated with the small or zero down payments being made by borrowers, especially on new home purchases.

Historically, if a borrower made a 20 percent down payment, the lender was protected because any potential lender losses would come out of the borrower's down payment. There was no risk to the lender.

Let's look at an example. A property sells for $200,000. The borrower makes a $40,000 (20%) down payment. A lender loans the borrower $160,000.

Purchase Price	$200,000
Down Payment	−$40,000
Loan Amount	$160,000

Say the value of the property goes down to $190,000 and the borrower loses their job. The borrower stops making payments and the lender begins foreclosure proceedings. The lender makes a credit bid at the foreclosure sale of $170,000 to recoup their loan amount and $10,000 in back payments and foreclosure costs.

An investor bids $170,001 and wins the bid. The lender receives $170,000. The borrower/owner receives $1. There is no lender loss. The borrower loses their $40,000 down payment/equity.

Let's use the same example and change the borrower's down payment to $10,000 (5%) of the purchase price. Now the loan amount is $190,000. The lender will require the borrower to pay for private mortgage insurance before the lender will agree to loan the borrower the $190,000.

Purchase Price	$200,000
Down Payment	−$10,000
Loan Amount	$190,000

Again the value of the property goes down to $190,000 and the borrower loses their job. The borrower stops making payments and the lender begins foreclosure proceedings. The lender makes a credit bid at the foreclosure sale of $200,000 to recoup their loan amount and back payments.

No investor will bid above the lender's credit bid because the property value is less than the lender's credit bid. The lender becomes the owner of the property. The private mortgage insurance will have to compensate the lender the difference between the $200,000 and whatever the lender can sell the property for as an REO.

Let's say the lender sells the property for $170,000. Then the private mortgage insurance will pay the lender $30,000. This will net the lender the $200,000 they have invested in the property.

Lender Sells Property	$170,000
Private Mortgage Insurance	+$30,000
Lender Nets	$200,000

PMI Short-Sales

PMI companies will participate in lender short-sales. Before agreeing to a short-sale, PMI companies may advance the defaulting borrower funds to bring the loan current. They will do this if the borrower makes a request and has the potential financial wherewithal to get back on their feet.

Of course, the borrower will have to sign a promissory note and agree to repay any PMI advanced funds. PMI companies will do this because this is cheaper than paying the lender an insurance claim.

In some instances, PMI companies will purchase the loan from the lender and modify the payments to the borrower. Again PMI companies will do this if they think it is less expensive for them in the long run. Rather than being out the cash for the insurance claim, by purchasing the loan they have made an investment.

In a short-sale, the PMI companies have to approve the short-sale as part of their agreement to reimburse the lender for any lender losses. Usually, private mortgage insurance will agree to pay the lender a specific amount comparable to a 20 percent borrower down payment.

Let's look at a PMI short-sale. We will use the same numbers from the last example. The original purchase price is

$200,000. The borrower makes a $10,000 down payment. The lender loans the borrower $190,000.

Purchase Price	$200,000
Down Payment	−$10,000
Loan Amount	$190,000

Again the value of the property goes down to $190,000 and the borrower loses their job. The borrower stops making payments and the lender begins foreclosure proceedings. If the lender conducted a foreclosure sale, they would make a credit bid of $200,000 to recoup their loan amount and $10,000 in back payments and foreclosure costs.

You arrive on the scene and make the borrower/owner a $135,000 short-sale offer. They accept and you present your borrower/owner-accepted offer to the lender. The lender submits the short-sale offer to PMI with a request to be reimbursed. PMI agrees to reimburse the lender $40,000. Will the lender accept your short-sale offer? Yes!

Let's look at the numbers. They will receive $135,000 from your offer. They will receive $40,000 from PMI. That is a total of $175,000 going to the lender.

Your Short-Sale Offer	$135,000
Private Mortgage Insurance	+$40,000
Lender Total	$175,000

For the lender, $175,000 cash now with a nonperforming loan off their books is much better for them overall compared to foreclosing on the property and having it become a lender real estate owned property. Once it becomes an REO, the lender must add fix-up costs, holding costs, and real estate commissions and closing costs to their expenses. If they could sell the property for its full market value of $190,000, they will net less than $175,000

Sales Price	$190,000
Fix-Up Costs	$5,000
Holding Costs	$4,000

| Commissions and Closing Costs | −$14,000 |
| Lender Net | $167,000 |

We think that PMI involved short-sales will increase exponentially over the next few years. This may actually make it easier to do short-sales because PMI will help the lender with their bottom line. This will improve our odds of having a lender accept our short-sale offers.

In the next chapter we will show you how to buy the mortgage in foreclosure at a short-sale price. Using this short-sale investment tactic, you bypass the property owner immediately. You are buying the mortgage paper. You are not buying the property!

CHAPTER 14

Buying the Mortgage in Foreclosure at a Short-Sale Price

You have the opportunity to make a significant amount of money by purchasing a promissory note from a lender before the foreclosure sale. You buy the lender's position in the note for a substantial discount from the face amount. In essence, you are making a short-sale deal with the lender. You also do not need the borrower/owner's permission to talk to the lender. You are approaching the lender directly and asking if they would be interested in selling their note.

This gives you three ways to make money. The first way you can make money is if the borrower makes up the default. This will give you a tremendous yield on your investment as the holder of the note. The next way you can make money is to continue the foreclosure process on the defaulting borrower. If no one outbids your credit bid at the foreclosure sale, you will wind up owning the property that is the security for the note. The third way you can make money is if someone bids above your credit bid. They have to pay you off in cash.

Approaching Lenders

We recommend you look for lenders that are private party lenders with limited experience in foreclosing on a promissory note. This is usually the case when the promissory note

167

holder is an out-of-the-area private party. These lenders are often unaware of the foreclosure process. They tend to have more motivation to sell than a local or professional note holder (commercial lender). We believe in the near future commercial lenders will participate in selling their mortgage notes at short-sale prices to help alleviate the pressure of their nonperforming loans.

Preparation

When you are contacting lenders, it is very important that you are well prepared to discuss the foreclosure situation. You should be able to make a presentation with as many specifics as possible. You need to know the details of the foreclosure procedure, the risks to the lender, and the options to minimize risks to the lender. In other words, put together a short-sale offer.

Obtain as much preliminary information as you can prior to the meeting. This should include copies of the notice of default, a property profile, and a report on taxes paid. The notice of default will be posted at your county courthouse. A title company will provide you property profiles and tax information. Take pictures of the property. Various shooting angles may be helpful in demonstrating to the lender that the property may have more risk than is desirable to the lender.

Complete a market analysis using comparable sales that have closed no more than three months prior to your lender appointment. Include questions for the lender to be answered at the scheduled meeting time.

Questions for Private Party Lenders

1. Are you aware of the foreclosure proceeding?
2. Do you know what you will have to do to protect your interest?
3. Do you have the resources to maintain the payments on the senior loans?

4. Are you willing to take the time and make the effort to foreclose?
5. Would you accept cash now rather than possibly nothing in the future?

The foreclosure procedure outline, showing the time for each phase and the borrower's options, will be a vital part of the presentation. Itemize the cost to repair, hold, and improve the property to salable standards. Include the cost for holding and marketing the property. Put together a presentation book that includes all of these figures and use it as a guide at the meeting with the lender.

Before you offer to purchase a promissory note, you should be certain that your evaluation of the property indicates that it is a smart investment. Also, you should always anticipate that the borrower may file for bankruptcy protection and stay the foreclosure (*stay* is the legal term a court uses to halt foreclosure temporarily).

Three Ways to Make Money

We said earlier that there are three ways to make money. The first way is to buy the note for a short-sale price and the borrower makes up the default. The second way you can make money is to continue the foreclosure process on the defaulting borrower and possibly end up owning the property. The third way you can make money is if someone bids above your credit bid at the foreclosure sale.

1. Buy the Note and the Borrower Makes up the Default

Let's create an example we can use for all three ways to make money. You find a holder of a first mortgage with an initial balance of $100,000. The interest rate is 8 percent annually. The loan is amortized for 30 years with a balloon payment due after five years. The monthly payment of principal and interest is $734.

Loan Terms

Note Amount	$100,000
Interest Rate	8%
Loan Term	30 Years
Monthly Payment	$734

The borrower makes payments for two years and gets three payments behind. The lender files a notice of foreclosure. The property is worth $115,000. You approach the lender and make a short-sale offer to buy the note at a discount. You offer the lender $78,000 for the note. This is a $20,260 or a 21 percent discount from the remaining balance of $98,260.

Dollar Discount

Remaining Balance	$98,260
Your Offer	−$78,000
Dollar Discount	$20,260

Percentage Discount

$20,260 ÷ $98,260	= 21%

You continue the foreclosure process. The borrower is now four months behind for a total of $2,936.

Payments Behind

Monthly Payment	$734
Months Behind	×4
Total Behind	$2,936

The borrower contacts you before the foreclosure sale and wants to make up the back payments. You agree to reinstate the loan for the $2,936. The borrower will resume making the regular monthly payment of $734.

There will be another 31 months of $734 payments for a total of $22,754. Then a final balloon payment of $95,804 is due. Let's see what kind of return you have received in less than three years. Remember you originally invested $78,000.

You initially received the four months of back payments to stop the foreclosure. This was $2,936. You then received 31 months of additional monthly payments. This was $22,754. Finally, you received a balloon payment. The balloon payment was $95,804. This is a total of $121,494.

Total Received

Back Payments	$2,936
Monthly Payments	$22,754
Balloon Payment	+$95,804
Total Received	$121,494

A $121,494 return on a $78,000 investment is a $43,494 profit.

Profit

Total Return	$121,494
Amount Invested	−$78,000
Profit	$43,494

A $43,494 profit on a $78,000 investment is a 56 percent total return on your investment. That works!

Total Return

$43,494 ÷ $78,000	= 56%

Figured on an annualized yield basis you made a 21 percent return on your $78,000 investment. We will take it!

2. Buy the Note and Foreclose on the Property

You buy the note from the lender at the short-sale price of $78,000. The borrower does nothing to make up the payments. You go through with the foreclosure sale.

At the foreclosure sale, you make your credit bid for the remaining loan balance, plus the four months of no payments received, plus the foreclosure costs. The remaining loan balance is $98,260. The four monthly payments are $2,936. The foreclosure costs are $1,700. This is a total of $102,896.

Credit Bid

Loan Balance	$98,260
Back Payments	$2,936
Foreclosure Costs	+$1,700
Credit Bid	$102,896

No one outbids your credit bid. You receive a trustee's deed to the property. You have now gone from being the lender on the property to the owner of the property.

We said the property is worth $115,000. You have your original $78,000 invested in buying the note. You have an additional $1,700 in foreclosure costs. You have a total invested in the property of less than $80,000.

Invested in Property

Original Investment	$78,000
Foreclosure Costs	+$1,700
Total Invested	$79,700
You have an equity position of	$35,300.

Equity Position

Market Value	$115,000
Total Invested	−$79,700
Equity Position	$35,300

A $35,300 equity position on a $79,700 investment is a 44 percent return on your investment.

Return on Investment

$35,300 ÷ $79,700	= 44%

You can rent or sell the property! Whatever fits your investment goals.

3. Buy the Note and Be Outbid at the Foreclosure Sale

The third way to make money is to buy the note at a short-sale price, conduct the foreclosure sale, and have your credit bid outbid by someone at the sale. We said your credit bid would consist of three parts. It would consist of the loan balance, the back payments, and your foreclosure costs.

Credit Bid

Loan Balance	$98,260
Back Payments	$2,936
Foreclosure Costs	+$1,700
Credit Bid	$102,896

Let's say someone bids $102,900. How do you make out? You have your original $78,000 investment plus your $1,700 in foreclosure costs for a total investment of $79,700.

Invested in Property

Original Investment	$78,000
Foreclosure Costs	+$1,700
Total Invested	$79,700

This means you have made $23,200 in 30 to 60 days.

Profit

Total Return	$102,900
Amount Invested	−$79,700
Profit	$23,200

A $23,200 profit on a $79,700 investment is a 29 percent total return on your investment.

Total Return

$23,200 ÷ $79,700   = 29%

Figured on an annualized yield basis, you made a 174 percent return on your $79,700 investment if the fore-closure sale was 60 days after you bought the note. You made a 348 percent return on your $79,700 investment if the foreclosure sale was 30 days after you bought the note. Now what do you think about buying a promissory note at a short-sale price?

Carrying a Mortgage

To complete this chapter, we want to give you the perspective of being in the position of selling a property and being a lender. You may be in a position to short-sale your own lending position so to speak and make an excellent return on your loan.

Let's say you sell a property for $250,000. The buyer assumes your $150,000 first mortgage. The buyer makes a $50,000 cash down payment. In order to complete the transaction, you agree to extend credit to the buyer in the form of carrying a second mortgage. You carry a $50,000 promissory note secured by a second mortgage on the property. You go from being an owner of the property to being a lender on the property.

Carrying a Mortgage

Assumed First Mortgage	$150,000
New Second Mortgage	$50,000
Down Payment	+$50,000
Sales Price	$250,000

Two years go by. The property is now worth $280,000. The buyer defaults on the first and second mortgages. You foreclose on your second mortgage. No one outbids your credit bid. You get the property back subject to the first mortgage.

In essence, you have done a short-sale on your second mortgage to yourself. It has been extinguished by the foreclosure sale. All that remains on the property is the first mortgage.

Extinguished Second Mortgage

First Mortgage	$150,000
Foreclosed Second Mortgage	+0
Total Mortgages	$150,000

You keep the original $50,000 down payment. You keep the two years' worth of payments you have received on your second mortgage, which amounts to $12,000. You get the benefit of two years of principal reduction on the $150,000, now \$147,000, first mortgage. Let's say it cost you \$9,000 to make up the back payments on the first mortgage plus pay the foreclosure expenses. How do you come out? As we said, the property is now worth \$280,000.

Total Net Return

Property Value Now	\$280,000
First Mortgage Now	−\$147,000
Your Equity Position	\$133,000
Cash Down Payment	\$50,000
Payments on Second Mortgage	+\$12,000
Total Return	\$195,000
Foreclosure Expenses	−\$9,000
Total Net Return	\$186,000

It looks like you came out smelling like a rose. You can keep the property for long-term wealth building or you can immediately resell it. Of course, you may want to carry a second mortgage for the new buyer, just in case they default!

In the next chapter we will show you how to buy property on the day of the foreclosure sale. There are two opportunities to make a good deal. You can make money buying property at the foreclosure sale itself if you know what you are doing or you can make a short-sale deal with the lender right up to the time of the sale!

CHAPTER 15

Buying at the Foreclosure Sale

For those of you who wait until the day of the foreclosure sale to go after a foreclosure investment opportunity, preparation is of the utmost importance. The bidding is often fast paced and you will have little time to make a decision. This may mean a poor outcome if you have not already inspected the property and made a title evaluation.

You need to come prepared in the financing department, too. Cash or cashier's checks are all that will be accepted by the trustee, sheriff, or other representative of the foreclosing party. You must strike a balance between bringing enough to win the bid and not bringing too much so that you go overboard and make a stupid purchase.

Gathering Information before You Bid

Two reports are available to assist an investor in getting the information about a property prior to making a bid. There is a *lot book report* and a *judgment lien report.* Check with your local title insurance company for their availability in your area.

They are the most economical way to get information about liens against the property short of getting a *preliminary title report,* which will cost you more.

A property profile will not give you that information, and you would be foolish to rely on a property profile alone. So, what is a lot book report or a judgment lien report?

Lot Book Report

The lot book report contains a record of everything that has been recorded against the property. Every property has a lien for property taxes. This is true even when the property taxes have been paid and the property tax account is current. Property taxes create a lien against the title to the property, which is called a lien that is due and not yet payable.

Any trust deeds or mortgages, which are the security devices for promissory notes or mortgage notes, respectively, and have been recorded against the property title, can be found in the lot book report. Also, any other liens or encumbrances that affect the title, such as easements, will show up.

Judgment Lien Report

The judgment lien report contains a record of any money judgments that have been recorded against the owner of record for the property. These can include IRS liens, civil lawsuit judgments, state income tax liens, personal property taxes, and family court matters.

You can go down to the county courthouse and research the recorded liens yourself, if you know where to look and what to look for. Ask for help from the clerks. They will usually be glad to oblige. We recommend you do this at least one time so you get a sense of the huge amount of materials that are recorded.

Why this information is important becomes apparent if you ignore it. Remember, when you are the winning bidder at the foreclosure sale and get title to the property from the foreclosing entity, you get the title subject to all the senior liens and encumbrances.

Let's say the holder of a third mortgage is foreclosing. The amount of the loan is $16,000. The borrower is in default in the amount of $2,500. The foreclosure expenses are $900. The trustee will open the bidding with a credit bid of $19,400.

You have valued the property at $140,000. You estimate that there is a $5,000 to $10,000 fix-up expense. At first glance, this looks like a very profitable foreclosure opportunity. If you can win the bid in the $25,000 to $30,000 range you are looking at a $100,000 or higher gain!

Opening Credit Bid

Loan Amount	$16,000
Default Amount	$2,500
Foreclosure Expenses	+$900
Credit Bid	$19,400

A first mortgage for $95,000 is in default in the amount of $7,300, however. A second mortgage for $25,000 is in default in the amount of $3,600.

First Mortgage	$95,000
Default Amount	$7,300
Second Mortgage	$25,000
Default Amount	+$3,600
Total	$130,900

It would not be a good thing to find out that the property has more than $150,000 in liens after we were the winning bidder. This would be a costly mistake!

When we talked about knowing value, we said that transferability was one of the four elements of value. (Demand, utility, and scarcity are the first three elements of value.) As the winning bidder, you become the proud owner of the title to the property. You have nothing of value if you cannot transfer a clear ownership title to another buyer.

Dry Run

As we have stated before, to gain the greatest advantage at the foreclosure sale, we recommend you do a dry run by attending one or two sales on property you are not interested in prior to the sale of the property in which you have an interest. This rehearsal will help give you the confidence you need to be successful at foreclosure sales.

Your observation of a foreclosure sale will be even more useful if you can witness a sale conducted by the same trustee, sheriff, or representative of the foreclosing party who will conduct the foreclosure sale on the property or properties in which you are interested.

How Foreclosure Sales Are Conducted

There are minor differences in the manner in which foreclosure sales are conducted throughout the United States. Your mission is to find out everything about the foreclosure sales in your particular area. For purposes of illustration, we will use trustee's sales in California as our guide.

Trustee's Sales in California

According to regulation, trustee's sales are held between 9:00 A.M. and 5:00 P.M. weekdays and may be held at any public place. Although many are held on the courthouse steps, the proximity to the courthouse is of little importance.

In fact, some lenders who want to discourage other people from bidding (usually private lenders who want to take the property back) will often schedule the foreclosure sale at some remote location in the county where the property is located just to keep the competition away.

Julian, California

We attended a foreclosure sale in Julian, California, for a property located in the city of San Diego. Julian is more than 50 miles from San Diego, but is in the same county. Needless to say, there were not many people at the foreclosure sale.

That was the point, however. The holder of a second trust deed was foreclosing. The amount of the second trust deed was $43,000. There was a small first trust deed on the property of $17,000. The property was worth $150,000 to $160,000.

The holder of the second trust deed wanted to make the credit bid and get title to the property. If no one else came to the foreclosure sale, he would wind up winning the bid. As a foreclosing second trust deed holder, he could step in and take over the first trust deed by just making the payments. There was almost a $100,000 equity position for the holder of the second if they could acquire the property in this manner.

Property Value	$155,000
First Mortgage	$17,000
Second Mortgage	−$43,000
Equity	$95,000

Unfortunately for the holder of the second trust deed, we had done our homework and knew what was going on. We came with cashier's checks. He was hoping to make a credit bid and win because no one else would be at the sale. Wrong!

Who Conducts the Foreclosure Sale?

The foreclosure sale will be conducted by a trustee (usually from a title insurance company, but a private individual can also conduct the sale). The trustee will cry the sale for the benefit of those in attendance. His cry (a description of the property to be sold) will be followed by a qualifying check of the bidders in attendance to verify that each has the ability to pay at least the opening bid.

The usual form of acceptable payment is cash or a cashier's check drawn on a California bank. The investor can find out in advance the trustee's requirements by contacting the trustee the day prior to the sale. Sometimes you can negotiate with the trustee to come up with a percentage of the winning bid at the foreclosure sale with the balance to be paid in 30 days.

When You Bid

Bring the amount you are willing to pay for the property and no more. Have the cashier's checks in various denominations so that you can provide the exact amount of your successful bid. Unless you have the checks in various denominations, a refund of your excess money could take several weeks.

Of utmost importance is that you do not share with anyone, or let anyone discover, how much money you have to bid on a property. This will weaken your chances for successful bidding because your competition can form a strategy to squeeze you out.

That is why we recommend you attend several foreclosure auctions to observe what goes on. It is not just important for you to observe the person conducting the foreclosure. It is also important for you to see how your competition operates.

Bidding Rings

You may discover that there is a bidding ring at your foreclosure sales. Although this may be illegal and unethical, you still must be prepared to encounter one.

A bidding ring conspires on who is going to get the winning bid. It works something like this. Three investors get together and agree on who is going to get what property. Investor 1 will get property A. Investor 2 will get property B. Investor 3 will get property C.

When property A comes up for bid, investor 2 and investor 3 will not bid against investor 1. If investor 1 encounters competition from you or other investors, however, investor 2 and investor 3 may start bidding. They do this for one of two reasons.

The first reason is to try to force you out of the bidding. They do this by trying to make you think there is too much competition for the property, hoping you will back off and wait for another property. Now one of the three conspirators will have the winning bid that is just higher than yours. If this is investor 2 or investor 3, they will defer to investor 1 and let investor 1 have the property.

The second reason is to try to bid up the price of the property and stick you with the winning bid. They try to get you so caught up in the frenzy and excitement of the bidding process, that you lose your cool. When you lose your cool, you get auction fever. The bidding ring is trying to give you a lethal case of auction fever. (We will talk about auction fever shortly.)

The point is once you have overbid on that first property, you may have taken yourself out of the game. Now you do not have the cash to bid on other properties coming up for sale. One and done. You are out of the bidding for the foreclosure sales for that month. That is exactly what the members of the bidding ring want to happen.

Even though you may be anxious to obtain the property, you must keep a poker face. Do not bid too early in the bidding. You will only drive the price up. In our experience, we have found that when we waited until the hammer went down a second time before we made our first bid, we experienced success.

Auction Fever

Auction fever occurs when you bring more than one buyer into a buying situation. In the normal real estate buying scenario, only one buyer at a time is making an offer on a property. If there are multiple offers, the buyers are not together in the same place, so each buyer's offer is unknown to the other buyers.

In a foreclosure auction, all the buyers are compressed in one place at the same time. The bidding is out in the open. Every offer is instantly known to the other buyers. This can create a bidding frenzy. We have seen people at foreclosure auctions actually faint! They became so excited during the bidding process, they passed out.

Bidding can be intoxicating. To coin a phrase, "You have to bid in moderation." If you notice you are coming down with auction fever, take deep breaths and stop bidding. We recommend you always take a friend or relative with you to protect against auction fever.

Buying at the Foreclosure Sale

Let's review. Foreclosure sales are conducted at a public auction. The highest bidder gets the property. The seller at the foreclosure sale is a trustee or representative of the lender. So the seller at the foreclosure sale is really an auctioneer. They are a professional seller. Yet, they do not have any financial stake in the property. They are just doing their job.

Once it gets to the foreclosure sale, the owner is out of luck. If you have not been able to help them or work out a purchase for their equity, the owner will lose all of their equity at the foreclosure sale. It is true that the owner can bid at the foreclosure sale, but how will that be possible? You must have cash to bid. If the owner had the cash to bid, they would not be in foreclosure!

Credit Bid

The opening bid is called a credit bid. The credit bid is put forward by the trustee, the sheriff, or the representative of the lender. The credit bid is the total of the remaining loan balance, payments in default, and any costs associated with the foreclosure sale.

If no one bids above the credit bid, then the lender winds up owning the property. Any bid made above the credit bid must be made in cash. Let's say the loan amount is $160,000 and the default amount is $10,000. Let's say the foreclosure sale expenses are $1,900. What would the opening credit bid be?

Opening Credit Bid

Loan Amount	$160,000
Default Amount	$10,000
Foreclosure Expenses	+$1,900
Credit Bid	$171,900

Winning the Bid

What if you bid one dollar more than the opening credit bid? When the hammer strikes the third time, and you are the highest bidder, *you own the property!* It is not a conditional contract, but one that you must immediately honor.

If you could buy the property at the foreclosure sale for $171,901, would that be a better deal than if you could have bought the property from the owner before the foreclosure sale for $179,000? The answer is that it depends. Although it certainly looks like getting the property at the foreclosure sale for $7,099 less is the better deal, maybe it is not the better deal. This is a price versus terms conversation.

When to Buy Property

Before the Sale	$179,000
At the Sale	−$171,901
Difference	$7,099

You may get a better price at the foreclosure sale, but you must come up with almost $172,000! Buying from the owner, you did not get as good a price—$179,000—but you only have $19,000 in the deal. Will that $7,000 lower price be worth tying up an additional $153,000?

When to Buy Property

Before the Sale		*At the Sale*
$179,000	Price	$172,000
$19,000	Cash in Deal	$172,000

Cash Difference

At the Sale	$172,000
Before the Sale	−$19,000
Cash Difference	$153,000

What about doing a short-sale the day of the foreclosure sale?

Short-Sale the Day of the Foreclosure?

This is where a short-sale makes more sense. If no one bids above the credit bid, the lender winds up owning the property. The lender is going to have to do property fix-up, including possible major repairs, sale preparation (makeready), and pay real estate commissions, not to mention how long it will take to market the property, find a buyer, receive an offer, and close escrow.

What if you could negotiate a short-sale deal with the lender the morning of the foreclosure sale for $135,000? Would that be a good deal for you? Yes, that would be a great deal for you. Why would the lender agree to your offer? Because it is in the lender's best interest to do so! A deal for $135,000 now looks better to the lender than waiting six to nine months to get maybe $145,000 to $150,000. And for you to come up with $135,000 is certainly better than you having to come up with $172,000.

Short-Sale Cash

At the Sale	$172,000
Short-Sale	−$135,000
Cash Difference	$37,000

What if you are unable to negotiate a short-sale the day of the foreclosure sale? What happens if no one bids above the lender's credit bid at the foreclosure sale? What if you are still interested in picking up the property? In the next chapter we will show you how to buy from the lender after the lender has taken the property back at the foreclosure sale. Remember, real estate lenders want to make real estate loans. They do not want to own real estate.

CHAPTER 16

Buying from the Lender after the Foreclosure Sale

W hat about buying from the lender after the foreclosure sale? Usually, the lender has the biggest financial stake in the property. After all, they made an 80 percent, a 90 percent, a 95 percent, a 97 percent, or even a 100 percent loan to the borrower to buy the property to begin with. Can you get a better deal from the lender once the property goes out of the lender's loan portfolio and into the lender's property portfolio? We think the answer is yes.

Lender's property portfolios are called real estate owned portfolios, or REOs for short. As we have said, with Department of Veterans Affairs (VA) REOs, some investors call them repos (short for repossessions). Real estate lenders are in the business of making real estate loans. Real estate lender's are not in the business of owning real estate. Although the lender wants to sell their REOs for as much as possible, they also want to move these REO properties as quickly as possible.

The REO Department

Our recommendation to you is to work with several lenders' REO departments and see what happens. You may find a niche working with one contact in one lender's REO department.

Once you can put together your first deal, you have a track record with that lender.

Your contact person will then start calling you with other deals, perhaps before they become open to the public. We say it this way: Contacts with people create opportunities. Contacts create contracts.

Price and Terms

There are only two major concerns for you as a real estate investor in a real estate deal: price and terms. The first major concern is the price for which you can get a property, after all is said and done. What is the rock bottom price the owner will take? What about the price when you are dealing with REOs? We have already said we think you can get a better deal from the lender after the foreclosure sale if the property does not sell. The lender is now the owner of the property. Getting rid of the property is now the lender's number one priority.

The second major concern is the terms for which you can get a property, after all is said and done. Usually, if a seller gets their price, the buyer gets their terms. If a buyer gets their price, a seller gets their terms.

For example, we will pay full price to a seller if we get our terms. What are our terms? We want to make no down payment. We want the seller to carry 100 percent of the financing. We want to make no monthly payments on the seller financing. If we get our price, we will give the seller their terms. If the seller accepts our wholesale price, we will pay them cash.

What about the terms when you are dealing with REOs? Ah, there is the rub. Are you going to have to pay cash? Are you going to have to qualify for a new loan? Are you going to have a combination of cash and new financing? Will the lender selling you the REO make you a great deal on the interest rate if you get a loan from them?

Preforeclosure Turned REO

We are going to take you through one of our deals. This deal started out in preforeclosure. We found a property listed with a broker in our target area. We called on the sign and spoke to the listing agent. She informed us that the owners were very motivated, and of course we liked hearing that. They were two months behind in their loan payments and were in pre-foreclosure. The agent then told us a separation had occurred between the husband and wife, with divorce imminent. We liked hearing that even better.

We began working with the owners and pursued the property through the posting of the notice of default. We were unable to make a short-sale deal with the lender. We went to the foreclosure sale on the courthouse steps.

We felt the price at which the lender made the credit bid was too high. So did the other investors at the foreclosure sale because no one bid. The lender had no alternative but to take the property back. Although the real estate lender is a professional seller, sometimes their own bureaucracy gets in the way of them making an effective deal. We did wind up finally making a deal with the lender after the property became an REO. But, we are getting ahead of ourselves. First things first.

Working with the Owner

The first thing we get from the owner is a written owner authorization to release information. We want to speak to the lender directly. This establishes a contact between the lender and us. Usually there is one person in the REO department who is assigned to a particular property. If not, we recommend you ask to speak with the same person every time. We did not realize how important this contact would be until much later.

The second thing we get from the owner is a written owner authorization for property access. We want to be able to get into the property without having to wait for the agent or owner to meet us. In this case, as with many foreclosures, the owners had moved out of the property.

Authorization for Property Access

July 22, 2006

To Whom It May Concern,

I (We), _____ (Owner's Name[s]), do authorize the
_____(Investor) and/or _____
(Investor) to access my (our) property at _____
_____. I (We) have given this authorization to _____
_____ so they may show prospective partners and/or
investors the property in order to complete funding of our sale.

I (We) have given _____ special instructions on
how to gain entrance to the property. This authorization for access to my
(our) property to _____ and/or _____
begins today and extends through _____.

Signed

_____ (Owner)

_____ (Owner)

Working with the Lender

When we contact the lender in the preforeclosure phase, we
are looking for two things. First, we want to establish a contact with someone working for the lender. Second, we want
something in writing from the lender so we know where we
stand moneywise with what the lender thinks they are owed.
This is called a *payoff quote schedule.*

Payoff Quote Schedule

Principal	$81,057.19
Interest	$3,720.37
Late Charges	$828.63
Returned Check Fee	$100.00
Foreclosure Expense	$1,000.00
Attorney Fee and Collection Cost	$855.00

Legal Fee	$200.00
Foreclosure Cost	$502.30
Foreclosure Fee	$549.29
Property Valuation Fee	$234.00
Property Inspection Fee	$7.75
Payoff Quote Fee	$10.00
Escrow Advance	+$3,944.60
Total Amount Due	$92,989.13

Is this an incredible list or what? Why is there a foreclosure expense for $1,000, a foreclosure cost for $502.30, and a foreclosure fee for $549.29? What are the differences between a foreclosure expense, a foreclosure cost, and a foreclosure fee? Only the lender knows. We think it is padding the bill.

In the nickel and dime category, how about the property inspection fee for $7.75 and the payoff quote fee for $10? Someone drove past the property, and the bank charged a fee. And did you catch the returned check fee for $100? Guess how many returned checks we are talking about? Two!

What is important about the payoff quote schedule is that it becomes the basis for the lender's credit bid at the foreclosure sale. In fact, this is very close to the actual credit bid this lender made at the foreclosure sale. Try as we might, we could not get this lender to budge in negotiations during this preforeclosure phase. We did not want to pay anywhere near $93,000 for this property. We did not find anyone else who wanted to pay that much for the property either.

Because the property was vacant, we were able to bring five different investor groups through it in a week's time. All were in the buy, fix, and flip business. This property definitely needed fixing. We had estimates from these five investor groups from a down and dirty $10,000 quick fix to $30,000 to $35,000 to do it right.

We also had prices that the investors would pay for the property in its as-is condition that ranged from $70,000 to $85,000. Surprisingly enough, the investor who said they would only put $10,000 into the property to fix it was the same investor who would only pay $70,000 for the property!

The retail value of the property fixed up would be $125,000. If you do the math it does not make sense. Once we pay the lender $93,000 for the property and spend $35,000 to fix it, we would have $128,000 in the deal!

You would have to sell the property for $3,000 above the retail price of $125,000 just to break even. We would be upside down in the deal. That was not very likely to happen since we had something to say about it. We told our contact person with the lender to forget about it!

Money in Deal

Lender Payoff	$93,000
Fix-Up Costs	+$35,000
Money in Deal	$128,000

Upside-Down Deal

Retail Value	$125,000
Money in Deal	−$128,000
Loss	($3,000)

Foreclosure Sale

Needless to say, this property went to the foreclosure sale. The lender made the credit bid of $93,567.23, and no one else bid. The trustee awarded the lender a trustee's deed, so the lender now owned the property.

The next day we called our contact person at the lender. We asked the REO department for how much they were going to sell the property? We found out they were listing the property with a real estate broker for $85,000 and that the price was negotiable!

The price had dropped more than $8,000 in one day. So much for getting a good deal at the foreclosure sale! But we already told you there are deals to be had once a property goes from the foreclosure sale back to the lender as an REO.

REO Offer

This property had now become a saga for us. We had found it in the preforeclosure phase and had tried to put together a deal with the owner. We were successful in getting the owner to work with us for zero net dollars to them. They had no equity in the property and just wanted our assistance in walking away. Our deal with the owner was contingent upon working something out with the lender.

We were going to flip the property to another real estate investor. We were trying to negotiate the lender down on their loan payoff so there would be some room for us to make a profit. In other words, we were trying to put together a short-sale! When the lender would not come off the $93,000 loan pay-off, we could not make a deal. No one said lending institutions were the smartest business organizations around. Something about one hand not knowing what the other hand is doing.

We approached the REO department and made an offer of $70,000, all cash, for the property. We did not want to buy the property for $70,000. We wanted to control the property for $70,000. We were not interested in coming up with $70,000 cash. We would leave that to the investor we assigned our contract to.

We submitted our offer through our contact person in the REO department. Our offering price was not a big bone of contention. The lender simply countered at $80,000. We countered their counteroffer with $73,900, and they accepted.

Our Offer

Lender List Price	$85,000
Our Offer	$70,000
Lender Counteroffer	$80,000
Our Counteroffer	$73,900

The lender was unwilling to allow us to assign our contract, however. We felt we would be able to work out an acceptable price to another investor, but if we could not get the lender to allow us to assign our contract, then we would have no deal.

No Such Thing as an Unassignable Contract

It has been our experience that there is no such thing as an unassignable contract. And some of the toughest contracts to assign are the ones from lenders after they have foreclosed on a loan and are reselling a property as an REO.

Real estate owned (REO) properties have been the source of some of our most profitable inventory. We were unwilling to let this deal go because of some attorney advising the lender. Lenders are just as hoodwinked as the rest of us when it comes to listening to attorneys. They allow their attorneys to put the dumbest things in their REO contracts. Remember, our position is that the purpose of the contract is to communicate.

Real estate attorneys, just like other attorneys, make money by keeping people from communicating. The following is actual verbiage taken from the lender's REO contract that their attorneys put in.

REO Real Estate Contract Excerpt

Buyer shall neither assign its rights nor delegate its obligations hereunder without obtaining Seller's prior written consent, which may be withheld in Seller's sole discretion. In no event shall an assignment relieve Buyer from its obligations under this Contract. Any other purported or attempted assignment or delegation without obtaining Seller's prior written consent shall be void and of no effect.

Needless to say, this paragraph was unacceptable to us. How did we get around this affront to our investor sensibilities? Did we get the lender's prior written consent before we wrote an offer? No, we did not. Our contact person gave us a clue.

We wrote the offer as trustees of a trust. As such, we were speaking a language the lender could understand. We did not know when we wrote the offer which trust was actually going to buy the property. The lender accepted our offer as Chantal

Carey or Bill Carey, trustees and/or assigns. We assigned the lender's unassignable contract within seven days after our offer was accepted for a $6,000 assignment fee.

Although this was a lot of work for the relatively small amount of money we made, we were happy. We had tried so hard to make this deal work at each of the four phases of the foreclosure process. To finally have something work in the last phase was very gratifying for us.

Our Profit

Sales Price to Investor	$79,900
Purchase Price	$73,900
Our Profit	$6,000

We must say here that dealing with REO lenders and their attorneys is very difficult. You must legitimately be a trustee before you can write and present contracts as one. We do not recommend this technique if you are just starting out in the foreclosure business.

For those of you who are more advanced or are trustees of trusts and want to consult with us for more information, contact us through our e-mail address, thetrustee@hotmail.com. You must fully identify yourself, or we will neither open the e-mail nor respond to it.

So if we had sold it below retail ourselves, rather than flip it as trustees to an investor, what would we have made? If the retail value is $125,000, and we like selling below retail for a quick sale, let's say we sold it for $110,000. We paid $73,900, did repairs for $22,000, which was the average of the three repair bids, and had closing costs of $1,000. We would have made $13,100.

Sold Retail

Sale Price	$110,000
Paid	$73,900
Repairs	$22,000
Closing Costs	−$1,000
Profit	$13,100

In the next chapter we will talk about bankruptcy and other problems. These are all areas you need to be aware of in order to avoid any potential pitfalls in your short-sale investing. Because we all know that knowledge is power, your obtaining this knowledge will go a long way toward you being powerful, despite whatever pitfalls you may encounter in the foreclosure arena.

CHAPTER 17

Bankruptcy and Other Problems

Ｗe will delve into four problems in this chapter. The first of these problems is an owner filing bankruptcy during your short-sale deal. The second problem is IRS tax liens. The third problem is the destruction of the improvements on the property before you close your short-sale. The fourth problem is any environmental issues that may affect the value of the property and ultimately your potential profit.

Bankruptcy may delay or stop you from closing on your short-sale. An IRS tax lien can affect the title to the property you are acquiring. The destruction of the property or environmental issues may make the property you are buying worth less than the amount you are paying for the property. In fact, the environmental issues could make the property just plain worthless. Let's discuss each of these potential problems starting with bankruptcy.

Bankruptcy

What do you do when the property owner files for bankruptcy? If the property owner files for bankruptcy, all of their assets are going to be frozen by the bankruptcy court. This includes any real estate holdings of the bankruptcy petitioner, whether they have equity in them or not.

Bankruptcy is a legal procedure established by federal law to assist debtors who cannot meet their financial obligations. The Founding Fathers of the United States were so opposed to the traditional British solution of throwing debtors into prison that they created an alternative solution.

Normally, you will discover that the property owner has filed bankruptcy in one of two ways. You may be notified of the bankruptcy because you have a relationship with the owner in your short-sale deal. Or you may discover that the property owner has filed bankruptcy from the title insurance company when you try to record your property deed at the short-sale closing.

Two Categories

Bankruptcies fall into two categories: liquidation and reorganization. In the United States, liquidation bankruptcies fall under Chapter 7 of the United States Bankruptcy Code. The debtor who takes this path ends up turning over all their nonexempt assets to the bankruptcy court. This can include their real estate holdings.

A court-appointed trustee then has the responsibility to liquidate (sell) the assets and distribute the proceeds to the existing creditors on a pro rata basis. Any debts that remain unsatisfied at that time are discharged and legally nullified. The trustee works for both the debtor and the creditors. It is the duty of the trustee to try to preserve the debtor's assets as much as possible to satisfy creditors.

Bankruptcies intended to assist the debtor with financial rehabilitation through reorganization come under the categories of Chapter 13 and Chapter 11. A Chapter 13 bankruptcy is intended for individuals with a regular source of income. We have found the owners with whom we do short-sales deals no longer have a regular source of income. That is why they are in financial trouble. A plan is proposed by which the debtor will continue to make payments on their debts and make up back payments with interest. A modified, extended schedule is often used to do this. This can include mortgage payments.

A Chapter 11 bankruptcy is used by corporations, partnerships, and those individuals who do not qualify for a Chapter 13 plan. The court procedures can be complex and lengthy. The cost of a Chapter 11 can be surprisingly expensive. New bankruptcy legislation went into effect in October 2005. The bottom line of the changes is the legislation has made it harder for people to qualify for a Chapter 7 bankruptcy wherein all of the petitioner's debts are eliminated. The emphasis now is for people to file a Chapter 13 bankruptcy and work out a repayment plan with their creditors. For this reason, the number of Chapter 7 bankruptcy filings is expected to decline significantly.

Foreclosure Stops

The moment a property owner in default files a petition for bankruptcy, foreclosure proceedings stop immediately. This is because a legal moratorium, called an automatic stay, is imposed by the bankruptcy court. It prevents creditors from pursuing any legal actions to enforce their claims against a debtor. Said in English, everything *stays* put until the bankruptcy court hears the case.

If a foreclosure sale is held after a bankruptcy petition has been filed, the foreclosure will be ruled null and void by the bankruptcy judge. Null and void are not good words to hear from a court. From the bankruptcy court's point of view, the foreclosure sale never took place!

A mortgage lender must first seek relief from the automatic stay in order to proceed. You must do the same in order to proceed with your short-sale. The Bankruptcy Act says the court must hear a lender's petition for relief from stay within 30 days. If the court fails to do so, the stay is automatically lifted.

Once the stay is lifted, the lender can proceed with their foreclosures. You can proceed with your short-sale. In a case in which you have purchased a mortgage in foreclosure from a lender and the borrower files a bankruptcy petition, you also must seek relief from the bankruptcy stay in order to proceed with your foreclosure.

Equity in Property

The amount of equity in the property will affect the judge's decision to grant relief from the stay. If there is significant value in the property being foreclosed or sold, the judge will not grant relief from the automatic stay. The hope is that some of that equity can be used to satisfy other creditors.

If there is very little equity in the property, the judge will usually grant a relief from the automatic stay and allow the foreclosing lender to proceed. In the case of your short-sale deal, you will be able to proceed to closing. Let's look at some examples. First we will look at a situation in which the owner has equity in the property. Then we will look at a situation in which the owner has little or no equity in the property.

The property owner has a property worth $75,000. The property is free and clear. You make an agreement with them to buy this property for $25,000.

Equity Purchase

Owner's Equity	$75,000
Your Offer	−$25,000
Equity You Pick Up	$50,000

The owner files for bankruptcy protection before you can close your equity purchase. The bankruptcy judge stays your purchase. After the judge determines there are creditors of the property owner and there is more equity in the property, the judge sets aside your purchase altogether.

The bankruptcy judge orders a bankruptcy sale of the property. The property owner has three creditors who have claims of $125,000 between them. What will happen to your equity purchase? Forget about it. It is totally gone. In fact, to add insult to injury, you are not even going to be granted creditor status for your $25,000 offer.

The highest bidder at the bankruptcy sale will receive clear title to the property. You are welcome to bid. It would be in your best interest to bid at least $25,000. That was what you were willing to pay for the property to begin with. If you want to bid more, you can.

How much more should you bid—$30,000, $40,000, $50,000? This is just like a foreclosure sale in which there are lots of people bidding. You have lost the luxury of being the only buyer. Let's say you win the bid for the property with a bid of $50,000. You may still make money on the deal, but the bankruptcy filing cost you $25,000.

How will the $50,000 you paid for the property be disbursed by the bankruptcy court? The $50,000 will be allotted to the three creditors with the $125,000 in claims.

Bankruptcy Sale

Winning Bid	$50,000
Funds for Creditors	$50,000

As you can easily see, the creditors will not receive all of their claims. To pay off $125,000, $50,000 is not going to make the creditors happy. They are going to receive 40 cents on the dollar.

Creditors Receiving

Creditors Receive	$50,000
Creditors Owed	$125,000
Percentage Received	$50,000 ÷ $125,000 = 40%

Short-Sale

What if the property owner has little or no equity in a property? This is usually the case if there is a loan on the property. Let's use the same value for the property of $75,000. This time there is a $60,000 loan on the property. Now the owner's equity position is only $15,000.

Owner's Equity

Property Value	$75,000
Loan Amount	−$60,000
Owner's Equity	$15,000

You make a short-sale deal with the owner to buy the property for $35,000. The owner's $15,000 equity position is wiped out. You are asking the lender to take a $25,000 loss.

Short-Sale Purchase

Loan Amount	$60,000
Your Offer	−$35,000
Lender Loss	$25,000

What happens if the owner files for bankruptcy protection before you close your short-sale because of those three same creditors who are owed $125,000? The lender is afraid of the bankruptcy court's authority to impose a short-sale (or cram-down) provision. The court can move to modify the terms of the mortgage or trust deed. This could include modifying the payment schedule to help the debtor or actually reducing the principal amount owed on the mortgage note.

The cram-down provision can only be used with reorganization types of bankruptcies (Chapter 11 and Chapter 13) in which the property plays a key role in the reorganization plan. In other words, the debtor must have a substantial equity position in the property and have a reliable source of income to qualify for a reorganization plan.

Neither of these conditions applies in this case. The owner has very little equity in the property and no reliable source of income. We petitioned the court to remove the automatic stay so that we could proceed with our short-sale. The bankruptcy judge lifted the stay for our deal.

There was no money in the property for the creditors to receive funds. The lender was already being crammed down by our short-sale offer. In fact, by the owner filing the bankruptcy, the lender was practically forced to accept our short-sale offer. Otherwise, the judge could have forced them to get even less in the deal.

Our experience with owners filing for bankruptcy and short-sales has been positive. It just may take a little more time to close your short-sale deal when a bankruptcy occurs. Bankruptcy is not necessarily a short-sale deal killer. We are going to complete our discussion about bankruptcy by mentioning a few twists, especially around the foreclosure arena.

Creative Debtors

Debtors have come up with some pretty creative ways to stall foreclosures. Maybe you thought that a person can only file a bankruptcy once every seven years? That is true of Chapter 7 liquidations, but it is not true with Chapter 11 and Chapter 13 reorganizations.

The United States law does not prohibit the act of filing bankruptcy, and it is the filing that brings on the automatic stay. Because of this, a growing number of debtors are using that loophole to further delay the foreclosure process. Many judges are now wise to this trickery and will quickly lift the new stay.

Bankruptcies Filed after a Foreclosure Sale

There have been cases reported in which a bankruptcy judge has overturned a foreclosure sale that occurred just prior to the filing of the bankruptcy petition. The judge may rule that the equity in the property could have been used to pay more creditors.

Because the United States Bankruptcy Code is a federal law, a debtor in any state can file a bankruptcy petition and stop the foreclosure process. If the bankruptcy petition is filed 15 days into the foreclosure, the foreclosure will resume on the 15th day after the automatic stay is lifted. In other words, the lender does not have to go back to the beginning of the foreclosure. They resume the foreclosure from its current point. Now let's see what happens if the IRS has placed a tax lien on the property.

IRS Tax Liens

An IRS tax lien is recorded against the taxpayer's property. The lien can be a junior or senior lien in relationship to other liens against the property. A lien is junior or senior to another lien based on the priority of when the lien was recorded. Earlier recording gives one lien seniority over another lien. The dollar amount of the lien does not determine its seniority.

If the IRS lien is senior to the lien of a foreclosing lender, the buyer at the foreclosure sale takes title to the property subject to the existing IRS tax lien. If you are doing a short-sale with this lender, you also would take title to the property subject to the IRS lien.

The tax lien can cloud the title to the property. You may find it difficult to get marketable title to the property while the lien is still in place. From our discussion of the elements of value, which included transferability, you may find the property difficult to resell. Sometimes you or your buyer can negotiate with the IRS to pay part of the lien to get it off the property. This is buying the tax lien for less than its face amount. You know, buying it for a short-sale price!

If the tax lien is junior to the foreclosing lender, the IRS must be notified and has the right to sell the property again within 120 days of the foreclosure sale. The IRS will do this if they think there is more equity in the property to get money to pay the tax lien. The IRS must pay back the investor who bought the property at the foreclosure sale, including their purchase money and expenses.

This can affect your short-sale with a lender who is in a senior position to an IRS lien. It is smart not to do any improvements or fix up the property until the 120 days has expired. If you do and IRS sells the property, you might want to be the new buyer to protect your investment! Of course, you may then wind up overpaying for the property. Now let's turn our attention to what happens to your short-sale when the improvements on the property are destroyed before you close your deal.

Destruction of Improvements

Though this is a fairly unlikely occurrence, it is possible. A fire, hurricane, tornado, or natural disaster could destroy the home or the improvements on the property. In 2003, we came very close to buying two properties on the Gulf Coast in Mississippi. The first was a six-story historic hotel in Biloxi. The second was an antebellum home in Pass Christian. Both were destroyed by hurricane Katrina in 2005. Sometimes the best deals you make are the ones you do not make.

This may not be as bad as it sounds, however. Most property owners carry casualty insurance. This will cover the cost of repairs. In some cases, the casualty insurance will pay off the outstanding liens if there is a total loss.

Sometimes the value of the land is greater than the value of the improvements on the land. Then, even if the improvements on the property are destroyed, the property retains sufficient value for you to have enough security to continue with your short-sale.

For some of you, this may be a research consideration. You may want to make sure that the land is worth more than the buildings. You can get a sense of the value of the land and the value of the improvements by looking at the allocation between the land and the improvements given by the taxing authority. This can be found on the property tax bill for the property. Finally, we will discuss environmental issues that can affect your short-sale.

Environmental Issues

This is a fairly rare occurrence. Your initial research will usually turn up any existing environmental issues. If there is an environmental problem in the area, keep away from these properties. Do not buy short-sale properties near commercial properties that could be contaminated.

There could be a problem with contamination if the site was formerly an auto repair shop, a dry cleaner, a gas station, a chemical plant, or a paint factory. Environmental issues are one of the reasons we recommended avoiding commercial properties for the average investor.

Foreclosing Decision

If you buy the mortgage in foreclose and wind up foreclosing and taking title to the property, you may be in for a big surprise. If the property is contaminated by toxic waste, hazardous chemicals, mold, radon gas, or lead paint, you may be liable for the cleanup costs as the property owner.

Of course this would be the case only if you foreclosed on your mortgage and acquired the deed to the property. No one says you have to foreclose on your mortgage. You could wait it out and see if the property is eventually cleaned up. Your mortgage is still a lien against the title to the property. Eventually, your mortgage may be paid off.

Other than doing your homework, there is not much more that you can do to avoid environmental problems. The best way to protect yourself from losing your personal assets to pay for environmental cleanup is to never own property in your name.

We suggest protecting yourself by incorporating your short-sale foreclosure investment business. Incorporation provides a shield for your personal assets. The most you will lose is the amount you have in the corporation's name.

You could also form a limited liability company (LLC). You could be a limited partner in a limited partnership. All of these structures provide you with personal asset protection.

The likelihood that any of the four problems we have discussed in this chapter will happen is relatively small. The property owner filing bankruptcy is the most likely occurrence statistically. An IRS tax lien is the second most likely occurrence. The destruction of the property improvements is less likely. An environmental problem is the least likely occurrence statistically.

In the next chapter we will give you important information on escrow, closing, and title insurance that you need to complete your successful short-sale. We will give you a warning right now: Never buy real estate without obtaining title insurance!

CHAPTER 18

Escrow, Closing, and Title Insurance

I n this chapter we will discuss the remaining elements of a successful short-sale. This has to do with you actually receiving the title to the property at the conclusion of your short-sale deal. Without the transfer of ownership from the property owner to you, there may not be much profit for you in the deal. A transfer of ownership revolves around escrow, closing, and title insurance.

Escrow

Escrow is a type of closing by which you and the property owner deposit money and/or documents with a neutral third party—the escrow holder. Whoever handles the closing of your real estate short-sale acts as an agent for you and the property owner. You and the property owner give the escrow holder instructions to hold and disburse documents and funds after certain conditions are met. The escrow holder acts as an impartial stakeholder and communicates with everyone involved in the transaction.

We recommend having an escrow because of the complexity of the closing process. The advantages of escrow are that the escrow holder is responsible for keeping documents and funds safe; making computations; receiving and distributing funds; carrying out the terms of the real estate contract; complying with federal, state, and local tax regulations; providing an accounting for the transfer process; and determining that all conditions have been satisfied.

An escrow is complete when all conditions listed in the escrow instructions are met and all acts specified in the instructions are performed. When an escrow is complete, the escrow holder disburses the funds and documents to close the escrow.

In its simplest format, an escrow would have the buyer put the money in the escrow account at the opening of the escrow. The seller would take the money out of the escrow at the closing of the escrow. The seller would put the deed to the property in escrow at the opening of the escrow. The buyer would take the deed to the property out of the escrow at the closing of the escrow.

Many things are occurring during the escrow period: termite inspections, physical inspections, money-partner inspections, geological inspections, title searches, procuring hazard insurance, obtaining financing, preparing loan documents, calculating closing costs, preparing deeds, and so on.

Escrow holders are usually prohibited from offering advice, negotiating with you and the property owner, revealing information about the escrow to people who are not a party to the escrow, and preparing or revising escrow instructions without the authorization of you and the property owner. So, how do you open an escrow?

Opening an Escrow

Consider choosing an escrow holder who is willing to take the time to explain what is happening and what you need to do. Choose a company that is located a convenient distance from where you live, so you can deliver and sign documents or money easily.

Depending on your area, the party that acts as the escrow holder may include independent escrow companies, escrow departments of lending institutions, title insurance companies, real estate brokers, and real estate attorneys. You may find that your area does a closing with an attorney rather than conducting an escrow.

After you select an escrow holder, open the escrow by following these steps:

1. Contact the escrow holder by telephone or in person. (We do not recommend your initial contact be by e-mail.)
2. Give the escrow holder all the relevant information regarding the sale.
3. Deposit the earnest money with the escrow holder, preferably in person or, if necessary, by certified mail.

The escrow officer collects the information necessary to prepare escrow instructions on a form called a *take sheet*. Data the escrow holder may need in order to prepare escrow instructions include the following:

1. Property description.
2. Parties to the transaction.
3. Proposed closing date.
4. Sales price.
5. Loans currently on the property (this is important in a short-sale).
6. Loans the buyer wants to put on the property.
7. Vesting of the title in the new owner.
8. Conditions of the title, such as the conditions, covenants, and restrictions.
9. Buyer's and seller's costs.

So what are escrow instructions about?

Escrow Instructions

Escrow instructions are the written agreement between you and the property owner that translates the real estate contract into a form used by the escrow holder to conduct and close the escrow. The escrow holder prepares the escrow instructions, using the take sheet as a guideline, so that the intent and conditions are identical to those in the contract. The escrow holder then asks you and the owner to read and sign the escrow instructions.

You should read the escrow instructions carefully. Make sure that the intent and conditions of the escrow instructions are identical to those in the purchase contract. Ask questions about items you do not understand or ones that do not appear to match those in the contract. Sign the escrow instructions only when you are satisfied that all items reflect exactly the terms of the purchase contract.

You and the property owner can make amendments (changes) to the escrow instructions. To do so, discuss the changes with the owner and obtain their agreement to make the change. Request that the escrow holder prepare documents for the change and send these documents to you and the owner. Sign the documents authorizing the change (the owner must also sign) and return the documents to the escrow holder. Now you are ready to close.

Closing

Understanding how the escrow closes can make you comfortable with a process many buyers and sellers find very confusing. Closing is the process by which funds and property title are transferred between you and the property owner. Although closing could be accomplished by you and the property owner simply getting together and exchanging money and documents, most real estate transactions today use an escrow type of closing. So how are prorations handled?

The Buyer's Day

The day the escrow closes is considered the *buyer's day*. What this means is that all the prorations of property taxes, hazard insurance, mortgage interest, and property rents are figured on this day. Prorations are the apportionment of charges owed on the property between the seller and the buyer.

Let's say the escrow closes on the 14th of the month. The seller is responsible for paying the property taxes, hazard insurance, and mortgage interest through the 13th day of the month. If the property is receiving rental income, the seller is entitled to receive a prorated share of the monthly rent through the 13th day of the month. This is because rents are paid in advance, usually on the first day of the month.

The buyer is responsible for paying the property taxes, hazard insurance, and mortgage interest starting on the 14th day of the month. If the property is receiving rental income, the buyer is entitled to receive a prorated share of the monthly rent from the 14th day of the month until the end of the month.

Quick Cash Caveat

Using our quick cash system, you may wind up receiving money directly from another real estate investor without going to a closing. You could be flipping a property before the closing. You could be assigning a purchase contract or an option contract to another investor, who will then go to a closing with a seller rather than you.

Closing Statement

Once the escrow closes, a *closing statement* is prepared by the escrow holder. In the United States all closing statements are referred to as a *HUD 1*. HUD stands for the Department of Housing and Urban Development. We have our escrow holder prepare an estimated HUD 1 to submit with our short-sale offer to the lender. That way, the lender can see how much money they will receive at the closing as a result of accepting our short-sale offer.

The closing statement is set up as a debit and credit accounting. The purchase price appears as a credit to the seller and a debit to the buyer. Any rental security deposits will be credited to the buyer and debited to the seller. Everything else will be prorated as a debit and a credit to the seller and buyer, respectively, based on the day of closing. Let's talk about title insurance next.

Title Insurance

If you buy property, get title insurance. Never buy property without title insurance. What is title insurance? Title insurance is a policy of insurance issued to you by a title company on completion of the final title search that protects your title to property against claims made in the future based on circumstances in the past.

Title insurance is especially important if you are investing in foreclosures. Liens and encumbrances against the property title tend to mushroom during the foreclosure process. In addition to the foreclosing lender, there may be tax liens, lawsuits, and other creditors with interests against the title to the property.

There are exceptions to our rule regarding buying title insurance. We know of an investor who bids on properties on the courthouse steps and does no preliminary research on either the condition of the title or the property. After he wins a bid, he goes inside the courthouse and checks the condition of the title using the public records. At the same time he has a partner do a drive-by inspection of the property.

He takes advantage of the two-hour window the foreclosing trustee allows for the winning bidder to produce the cash or cashier's checks. If the property looks like a bomb, he backs out of the deal. If he discovers problems too great for him to handle with the title to the property, he backs out of the deal.

This is found out through a title search.

Title Search

A *title search* is an examination of information recorded on a property, or on the owner of the property, at the county recorder's office in the county where the property is located. The examination verifies that the property will have no outstanding liens or claims against it to adversely affect a buyer or lender when the title to the property is transferred to a new buyer or pledged as collateral for a real estate loan.

When you are buying property, especially a foreclosure property, it is always a good idea to get a preliminary title report from a title insurance company. The preliminary title report is usually produced by the title company during the escrow or closing. The purpose of the preliminary report is to make everyone—buyer, seller, lender, escrow holder, title company—aware of the condition of the title involved in the transaction. Let's talk about the types of title policies—the owner's, buyer's, and lender's policies.

Owner's Policy

An owner's policy of title insurance protects the owner of record from claims against the title brought by other parties. If a claim arises and you have title insurance, and any monetary damages are to be paid, the title insurance company will pay them. By the way, the seller or buyer can pay for the owner's policy. You want to get the owner's policy of title insurance on all your short-sale deals. This will protect your short-sale investment from potential disaster.

Buyer's Policy

A buyer's policy of title insurance protects the buyer of real estate. The buyer's policy is similar to the lender's policy in that it protects the buyer for matters beyond what is in the public record. Although the buyer becomes the owner and is protected by the owner's policy, a buyer may feel they want extended coverage. We recommend getting buyer's coverage any time you are involved in a foreclosure transaction.

Lender's Policy

A lender's policy of title insurance protects the real estate lender beyond matters of public record. There may be unrecorded liens against the title. A lender wants to be protected against everything because they have so much money loaned on the property. Typically, the lender makes the buyer who is using the loan proceeds to complete the purchase of the property pay for the lender's title policy.

Short-Sale Closings

We recommend you find an escrow holder who is adept at handling short-sale closings. This becomes very important if you are using the same escrow holder to handle the buying portion of the short-sale property and the simultaneous selling portion of the short-sale property. In other words, if you are flipping your short-sale.

We know of a situation in which the escrow holder made the egregious error of telling the short-sale lender about the new lender financing the property for $45,000 more than the short-sale lender was receiving. Needless to say, there was hell to pay. People lost their jobs, and the investor lost their short-sale deal.

We will conclude the book with a chapter on flipping your short-sales for a quick profit.

CHAPTER 19

Flipping Your Short-Sales

Flipping is a two-step process. The first step is to tie up a property. This is otherwise known as making an offer. The second step is to find a buyer. This is known as making money on your deal. This is the purpose of flipping and is the quick cash strategy in action.

When you flip short-sales, you use the same techniques as flipping non-short-sales, but with a few modifications. In this chapter we will talk about the flipping techniques for all properties and give you the particulars for flipping short-sales.

We will introduce you to our real estate investment axiom: Buy the property first, then get the financing. The short-sale corollary to this axiom is buy the short-sale first, then get a buyer. When you follow these axioms, it makes it easier to write offers. As we have said, writing an offer is the way to tie up a property. When you tie up a property, you control a property.

Tying up a Property

In the 1990s, when we traveled the country teaching real estate investors Robert Allen's Nothing Down seminars, we blew them away with buy the property first, then get the financing. In city after city, people told us we could not buy real estate this way.

We told them to try it our way and report back to us what happened. Lo and behold, from Seattle to Orlando, from Los Angeles to Baltimore, from Chicago to Dallas, our students

215

found that they could indeed buy the property first, then get the financing.

Mind-Set

Most, if not all, retail buyers (home buyers) have this mind-set: How much money do I have to put down and how much of a monthly payment can I afford? With this mind-set, they go to a lender to get prequalified for a real estate loan.

What the real estate lender says determines how much of a house the home buyer thinks he or she can afford. Of course, being prequalified means nothing once you actually apply for a loan. You can be prequalified for a $200,000 loan and actually wind up receiving only a $175,000 loan at closing.

You are a real estate investor, not a home buyer. You are a wholesale buyer of real estate. You are going to do things differently. Everyone, except us, will tell you to get your financing first, then buy the property. Here are some examples of deals we have done.

Buy the Foreclosure First, Then Get a Buyer

Example 1

Buy the Foreclosure First

We found a four-bedroom, two-bathroom, single-family home. The property was headed to foreclosure. The retail value of the property was $159,000. The seller had an assumable VA loan with a remaining balance of $129,000. The seller was $3,000 behind in his payments. The seller's equity position was $27,000.

Seller's Equity Position

Retail Value	$159,000
1st Mortgage	$129,000
Back Payments	−$3,000
Seller's Equity	$27,000

The seller had a $27,000 equity position in a property that was worth $159,000. This meant that the seller had a 17 percent equity position in the property.

Seller's Equity Percentage

$27,000 Equity Position ÷ $159,000 Retail Value = 17%

According to our guidelines, because the seller's equity position exceeded 15 percent, we were interested in buying the seller's equity. We set up an appointment with the agent and the seller. When the seller's agent asked us what we were prequalified for, this was our response (and will be yours). We told the agent that we were real estate investors. If the property met our parameters, we had the financial resources, along with our money partners, to buy the property.

We met with the seller and their agent. We made the foreclosure options presentation. At the end of our presentation, the seller said they would like to sell us their property. We offered the seller no money down and agreed to take over payments on the loan and make up the $3,000 in back payments. The seller accepted our offer. The seller would pay their agent the real estate commission.

We did not have to qualify for a new loan. We did not have to qualify to take over the seller's VA loan. We did not have to come up with a down payment. We made an offer that worked for us. We let the seller decide whether to accept our offer. We and you may not have accepted our offer. Why the seller accepted our offer was the seller's business.

Then Get a Buyer

We now had a property available to flip. Only by making an offer can you start the process of flipping a property. We flipped the property for $139,000 within two weeks to a retail buyer who was going to live in the property. Why did we flip the property for so cheap a price? Our strategy is quick cash. Could we have waited and perhaps gotten a higher price? Yes, but our quick cash strategy embraces the homily "A bird in the hand is worth two in the bush."

The buyer was going to assume the VA loan on the property. The buyer was actually a veteran. They were going to use their VA eligibility to assume the loan. The buyer was very happy to get a good deal. The seller was happy because they were out from under the foreclosure with no deficiency judgment hanging over their heads. We were happy because we had made $7,000.

Our Profit

Sales Price	$139,000
Purchase Price	$129,000
Back Payments	−$3,000
Profit	$7,000

Example 2

Buy the Foreclosure First

We found a three-bedroom, two-bathroom, single-family home with a pool. The property was in foreclosure. The lender had sent the first formal notice of default letter. The sellers were in a panic.

The retail value of the property was $210,000. The first mortgage on the property had a remaining balance of $155,000. The sellers were $9,000 behind in their payments. The seller's equity position was $46,000.

Seller's Equity Position

Retail Value	$210,000
1st Mortgage	$155,000
Back Payments	−$9,000
Seller's Equity	$46,000

The seller had a $46,000 equity position in a property that was worth $210,000. This meant that the seller had a 22 percent equity position in the property.

Seller's Equity Percentage

$46,000 Equity Position ÷ $210,000 Retail Value = 22%

Again, according to our guidelines, because the seller's equity position exceeded 15 percent, we were interested in buying the seller's equity. We offered the sellers $10,000 for their equity in the form of a promissory note secured by a second trust deed on the property. The promissory note was a straight note for three years. This means there were no payments until the final balloon payment of principal and interest at the end of the three years.

We also agreed to pay the $9,000 in back payments and reinstate the loan. The total cash out of our pocket was $9,000. Remember the $10,000 we offered the seller for his equity was a promissory note and not cash. We were not worried about this promissory note because we were going to flip the property.

Then Get a Buyer

We flipped the property for $185,000. The buyer was a real estate investor who was planning to rent the property. They assumed the first mortgage of $155,000 from the lender and our second mortgage of $10,000 to the seller.

We were now off the hook to pay the seller on the $10,000 second mortgage. Because the $10,000 second mortgage had no payments, the real estate investor would be able to have a positive cash flow.

How did we make out on this deal? We invested $9,000 cash and received our money back plus an $11,000 profit. The seller avoided foreclosure and had $10,000 plus interest coming his way three years down the road. The investor was happy because they got a good deal.

Our Profit

Retail Value	$185,000
1st Mortgage	$155,000
2nd Mortgage	$10,000
Back Payments	−$9,000
Profit	$11,000

Some of you are thinking, why did you guys not hold onto the property like the investor you flipped the property to, rent it out, and have a positive cash flow? That is good thinking if you are using the long-term wealth-building strategy. We were using the quick cash strategy, so landlording was not on our agenda.

Example 3

Buy the Foreclosure First

Early on in our real estate investing career, we tied up a three-bedroom, three-bathroom, single-family home with a pool. The seller was in preforeclosure. We negotiated a deal with the seller and bought their equity. We then spent $8,000 fixing up the property.

We are presenting this example here as our coaching you on what not to do. This was not one of our finest hours. We were still in the more traditional mind-set of trying to make everyone in the deal happy. By the time this deal blew-up, no one was happy.

Then Get a Buyer

We found retail buyers who said they were in love with the house. To make the deal work, we agreed to repaint the inside of the house, which we had already repainted, the colors the buyers wanted.

We also agreed to run a natural gas line to the utility room so the buyers could use their gas dryer. Finally, we had a tree removed from the pool area because the buyers were concerned that the roots were going to crack the bottom of the pool.

Can you guess what happened? The buyers came down with a disease all retail buyers get during the course of a real estate transaction. Some buyers get a mild case of the disease. Some buyers get a severe case of the disease. Unfortunately for us, these particular buyers came down with a terminal case of the disease.

Buyer's Remorse

What is this dreaded disease? Buyer's remorse! Every buyer experiences the onset of the disease once their offer is accepted by the seller. Even as a real estate investor, you will experience buyer's remorse. There is no known antidote or medication. The disease just has to run its course.

The symptoms of buyer's remorse usually strike at night, when a buyer is about to go to sleep. Sometimes the symptoms strike after the buyer has fallen asleep and they awaken as if from a nightmare.

The buyers start having doubts about the purchase. Are they doing the right thing? Should they look at more properties? Did they offer too much? Can they really afford the monthly payments? Is the house big enough? Is the house too big?

They start to sweat. They get out of bed and get a drink of water. They go back to bed, but they cannot fall asleep. The questions begin swirling again in their heads. What if they do not qualify for a loan? What if they *do* qualify for a loan? Who is going to take care of the pool? What if the pool does leak?

In our case, three weeks after we had accepted the buyers' offer and three days after we had finished repainting, installing the gas line, and removing the tree, the buyers backed out. Their case of remorse became terminal for them and for us. Our deal was dead.

Bottom line: Provide allowances for the work to be done after closing, if you must, to make the deal work, but do not spend your time or money on it before closing. Oh yes, and our profit on this deal? Do not ask. You got the point, right?

Example 4

Buy the Foreclosure First
The other problem with retail buyers is they usually do not pay cash for their real estate purchases. They have to qualify for and obtain a loan from a real estate lender. This means you will have to wait longer to get your money. Forty-five days is a fairly standard closing period from the time an offer is accepted to getting a loan processed and funded.

In the case of a government-insured loan or a government-guaranteed loan such as Federal Housing Administration (FHA) loans or Veterans Administration (VA) loans, it may take anywhere from 45 to 75 days to fund the loan and close the escrow!

Then Get a Buyer

Again, early on in our real estate investing career, we tied up a three-bedroom, one-and-a-half-bathroom condo that was in preforeclosure. We bought it for nothing down and took over the seller's existing loan. We flipped the condo to a retail buyer who made an FHA offer to us for $89,000. This looked like a sure moneymaker for us because we only had $2,000 in the property for back payments on the loan.

Our Profit

Sales Price	$89,000
Purchase Price	$77,000
Back Payments	−$2,000
Profit	$10,000

The escrow was to close in 45 days or sooner. When it finally closed after 79 days, we had several unexpected surprises! The first surprise was that the deal actually closed. That was a nice surprise. The other surprises were not so nice.

We had almost three months of interest due on the old loan. We had almost three months of property taxes to pay. And we had almost three months of homeowner's association dues to pay as well. These costs were really starting to add up.

The coup de grace was the four discount points we had to pay for the buyer on the $84,000 FHA government-insured loan. Each discount point was 1 percent of the loan amount. This amounted to $840 per point! We had no idea this was going to be so expensive. Needless to say, we were not happy with what happened to our $10,000 potential profit.

Actual Profit

Potential Profit	$10,000
Loan Interest	$1,540
Property Taxes	$750
Homeowner's Dues	$353
FHA Discount Points	−$3,360
Actual Profit	$3,997

Wholesale Buyers

We actually prefer flipping our foreclosure properties to wholesale buyers. Wholesale buyers do not get buyer's remorse. (Well maybe a little bit.) We know what some of you are thinking: How can you make any money flipping real estate to wholesale buyers? Don't wholesale buyers want to pay a wholesale price?

We do flip our foreclosure investments at a wholesale price to wholesale buyers! We are not greedy about it. We prefer to do many smaller deals and make a quick profit rather than one or two big deals that are very time-consuming and entail more risk.

We have come to appreciate that being successful real estate investors is strictly a numbers game. Although we prefer to flip our foreclosures to other investors for all the reasons we just talked about, we are still smart business people. Our marketplace is retail and wholesale buyers. The more buyers you have in your potential pool, the more likely you will be able to flip your foreclosures successfully. So what do you do with your short-sale deals if you are not into long-term wealth building?

Flipping Your Short-Sales

Our short-sale axiom is to buy the short-sale first, then get a buyer. Actually, buying the short-sale and finding a buyer to flip it to are simultaneous activities. Up until 2005, we were able to flip our short-sales in a simultaneous closing. We would make a deal with the property owner in distress who had little or no equity in their property to do a short-sale. We would then present our short-sale offer to the lender. As the lender was accepting our short-sale deal, we lined up potential retail buyers to flip the property to.

This all changed with the new lending laws. Now you must have two separate and distinct transactions in your short-sale investing. You must go in and cash out the short-sale lender in order to get title to the property. Then you can turn around and immediately sell your short-sale property to a new buyer.

You can still flip your short-sale contract by assigning the contract to another short-sale buyer. Just be aware of the caveat we have made regarding lenders being unreceptive to assigning any real estate contracts let alone a short-sale contract.

As with any real estate investing, the good deal is the most important requirement. Finding the money to fund your good deal is the easy part. We know money investors who will loan cash to us to fund our short-sale deals at 15 percent interest and three points. Given that we need the money for 30 to 60 days, the actual cash cost for the financing is fairly minimal in comparison to the amount of money we recoup once we sell the property to a retail buyer.

We will give you one final example so you can see what we mean. We had a short-sale offer accepted for $150,000 cash. We wanted to commit only $100,000 of our cash. We borrowed $50,000 from an investor for 60 days at 15 percent annual interest.

Borrowing Funds

Short-Sale Price	$150,000
Our Cash	−$100,000
Borrowed Funds	$50,000

This cost us $1,250 in interest and $1,500 in points for a total of $2,750.

Interest and Points Cost

Interest	$1,250
Points	+$1,500
Total	$2,750

We sold this property for $209,000. We made $56,250 after repaying the loan, the interest, and the points.

Profit

Sale Price	$209,000
Our Cash	$100,000
Loan	$50,000
Interest and Points	−$2,750
Profit	$56,250

We hope this last example will make some lightbulbs go on for some of you. Short-sale investing is only going to get more lucrative. By getting involved in this exciting real estate foreclosure arena now, you will be insuring a bright financial future. We predict that because some of you have read this book and become short-sale foreclosure investors, the number of millionaires in the world just went up!

CONCLUSION

Congratulations on completing *Make Money in Short-Sale Foreclosures: How to Bypass Owners and Buy Directly from Lenders.* We know you have a lot of material to digest. Our hope is that we have stimulated your interest in making money in short-sale foreclosures.

Our recommendation is for you to go back to the areas that are of the most interest for you. Please reread them. Then get started. Look at property. Schedule an appointment with an owner in preforeclosure. Make a foreclosure options presentation. Write a short-sale foreclosure offer! Our point is: Do something! Make some money.

We are always coming up with more creative possibilities for investments and problem solving. So, as we bid you farewell, we have this to say to you: Get creative! Pull a group of people together and contact us for a seminar.

Are you a lone ranger right now? You will not be for long when you start investing in short-sale foreclosures. Meanwhile you can e-mail us for fee-based consulting. We are always open to new possibilities, so let us know if you need a partner. Get out there and do something *now!*

Let us know what did or did not work for you. We want to hear about your experiences in the short-sale foreclosure arena. You can contact us through our publisher, e-mail us at thetrustee@hotmail.com, or write to us at PO Box 274, Bedford, TX 76095-0274.

Remember to watch for more of our Win Going In! series. The first book in the series was *The New Path to Real Estate Wealth: Earning Without Owning.* The second was *Quick Cash in Foreclosures.* The third book was *Make Money in Real Estate Tax Liens: How to Guarantee Returns Up to 50%.* This book is the fourth, and watch for the fifth in this Win Going In! series due out in autumn 2006. God bless y'all!

Chantal & Bill Carey

Deeds Chart

For use in the United States. All other areas please check with
your local law agent.

G = Grant deed is a deed using the word grant in the clause
that awards ownership.This written document is used by
the grantor (seller) to transfer title to the grantee (buyer).
Grant deeds have two implied warranties. One is that the
grantor has not previously transferred the title.The other
is that the title is free from encumbrances that are not
visible to the grantee. This deed also transfers any title
acquired by the grantor after delivery of the deed.

W = Warranty deed is a deed in which the grantor (usually
the seller) guarantees the title to be in the condition
indicated in the deed.The grantor agrees to protect the
grantee (usually the buyer) against all claimants to the
property.

* = Special deed.

STATE	DEEDS	STATE	DEEDS
Alabama	W	Delaware	G
Alaska	W	Washington, D.C.	G
Arizona	G	Florida	W
Arkansas	G	Georgia	W
California	G	Hawaii	W
Colorado	W	Idaho	W
Connecticut	W	Illinois	G,W

(continued)

STATE	DEEDS	STATE	DEEDS
Indiana	W	North Carolina	W
Iowa	W	North Dakota	G,W
Kansas	W	Ohio	W
Kentucky	W	Oklahoma	G
Louisiana	W	Oregon	W
Maine	W	Pennsylvania	G
Maryland	W	Puerto Rico	*
Massachusetts	W	Rhode Island	W
Michigan	W	South Carolina	G,W
Minnesota	W	South Dakota	W
Mississippi	W	Tennessee	W
Missouri	W	Texas	G
Montana	G	Utah	W
Nebraska	W	Vermont	W
Nevada	G	Virginia	G
New Hampshire	W	Washington	W
New Jersey	G,W	West Virginia	G
New Mexico	W	Wisconsin	W
New York	G	Wyoming	W

A PPENDIX B

Loans Chart

For use in the United States. All other areas please check with your local law agent.

M = Mortgage, a contract by which you promise your property without giving up possession of the property to secure a loan. You also retain title to the property.

TD = Trust deed, a contract used as a security device for a loan on your property, by which you transfer bare (naked) legal title with the power of sale to a trustee. This transfer is in effect until you have totally paid off the loan. In the meantime you have possession of the property.

* = Mortgage preferred; trust deed also valid.

** = Trust deed preferred; mortgage also valid.

*** = Use note to secure debt.

STATE	DEEDS	STATE	DEEDS
Alabama	M,TD	Florida	M,TD
Alaska	M,TD	Georgia	***
Arizona	M,TD	Hawaii	M
Arkansas	M	Idaho	M,TD
California	TD	Illinois	M,TD
Colorado	TD	Indiana	M,TD
Connecticut	M	Iowa	M,TD
Delaware	M	Kansas	M
Washington, D.C.	TD	Kentucky	M,TD*

(*continued*)

STATE	DEEDS	STATE	DEEDS
Louisiana	M	Ohio	M
Maine	M	Oklahoma	M,TD
Maryland	M,TD	Oregon	M,TD
Massachusetts	M	Pennsylvania	M
Michigan	M	Puerto Rico	M
Minnesota	M	Rhode Island	M
Mississippi	M,TD**	South Carolina	M,TD
Missouri	TD	South Dakota	M
Montana	M,TD*	Tennessee	TD
Nebraska	M,TD	Texas	TD
Nevada	M,TD	Utah	M,TD
New Hampshire	M	Vermont	M
New Jersey	M	Virginia	M,TD*
New Mexico	M,TD	Washington	M,TD
New York	M	West Virginia	TD
North Carolina	M,TD	Wisconsin	M
North Dakota	M,TD	Wyoming	M,TD

A PPENDIX C

Contracts and Paperwork

PURCHASE CONTRACT FOR REAL ESTATE AND DEPOSIT RECEIPT

This is meant to be a legally binding agreement. Read it carefully.

City:_____ State:_____ Date:_____

Received from _____, the buyer, the sum of $_____

shown by ☐ cash, ☐ cashier's check, ☐ personal check, or ☐ _____

payable to _____

to be held uncashed until this offer is accepted as deposit toward the purchase price of

_____ dollars ($_____)

for the purchase of property located in the state of _____,

county of _____, city of_____,

and known as _____

CAPTIONS: The headings and captions in this document are to make reference easy and are not intended as a part of this agreement.

1. **FIXTURES:** All permanently installed fixtures, fittings, and plantings that are attached to the property or for which special openings were made, as well as their controls, if any, are included in the purchase price, including _____

    _____

    except _____.

2. **PERSONAL PROPERTY:** The following items of personal property, free of liens and without warranty, are included: _____

    _____

3. **PROPERTY CONDITION:** Seller guarantees that through the date seller makes possession available to buyer

    A. The property and improvements, including grounds and landscaping, shall be maintained in the same condition as on the date of acceptance of the offer;

    B. The roof is free of all known leaks;

    C. All permanently installed fixtures and fittings, as well as their controls, if any, are operative;

    D. Seller shall replace any cracked or broken glass;

    E. And _____

    F. Except _____

    _____

4. **SELLER REPRESENTATION:** Seller guarantees that until the date escrow closes that seller knows of no violation notices of codes, laws, or other regulations issued or filed against the property.

5. **SUPPLEMENTS:** The attached documents are incorporated in this document:

    ☐ _____

    ☐ _____

    ☐ _____

    ☐ _____

    (continued)

Buyer and seller acknowledge receiving a duplicate of this page, which is page 1 of ____ pages.

Buyers' initials (_____) (_____)   Sellers' initials (_____) (_____)

PURCHASE CONTRACT FOR REAL ESTATE AND DEPOSIT RECEIPT

Property known as _____

6. **ESCROW:** Buyer and seller shall deliver signed instructions to _____
_____, the escrow holder, within _____ calendar days of
acceptance of the offer. The offer shall provide for closing within _____ calendar days of acceptance.
Escrow fees to be paid as follows: _____
_____

7. **OCCUPANCY:** Buyer ☐ does ☐ does not intend to occupy property as buyer's primary
residence.

8. **POSSESSION:** Possession and occupancy shall be delivered to buyer ☐ on the close of escrow,
☐ no later than _____ days after the close of escrow, or ☐ _____

9. **KEYS:** Seller shall provide keys and/or other means to operate all property locks and alarms, if any,
when possession is available to the buyer.

10. **FINANCING:** This agreement depends on the buyer obtaining financing.

   A. DILIGENCE AND GOOD FAITH - Buyer agrees to act with diligence and
      good faith to obtain all appropriate financing.

   B. DEPOSIT is due on acceptance and is to be deposited into _____
      _____ in the amount of $_____

   C. INCREASED DEPOSIT is due within _____ days of acceptance and is to be
      deposited into _____ in the amount of $_____

   D. DOWN PAYMENT BALANCE is to be deposited into _____
      _____ on or before _____ in the amount of $_____

   E. NEW FIRST LOAN - Buyer to apply for, qualify for, and obtain new first loan
      in the amount of .... $_____
      payable monthly at approximately $_____
      including interest at origination not to exceed _____ %
      ☐ fixed rate ☐ other _____
      all due _____ years from the date of origination.
      Loan fee at origination not to exceed $_____ .
      Seller agrees to pay a maximum of _____ FHA/VA discount points.
      Additional terms:_____
      _____
      _____

   F. EXISTING FIRST LOAN - Buyer to ☐ assume ☐ take title subject to
      an existing first loan with an approximate balance of .... $_____
      payable monthly at $_____ including interest at _____ %
      ☐ fixed rate ☐ other _____
      Fees not to exceed $_____ . Disposition of impound account ___

      Additional terms: _____
      _____
      _____

(continued)

Buyer and seller acknowledge receiving a duplicate of this page, which is page 2 of ____ pages.
Buyers' initials (_____) (_____)   Sellers' initials (_____) (_____)

PURCHASE CONTRACT FOR REAL ESTATE AND DEPOSIT RECEIPT

Property known as _____

10. FINANCING:

   G. **NOTE SECURED BY TRUST DEED** - Buyer to sign a note secured by a
      ☐ first, ☐ second, ☐ third trust deed in the amount of .... $_____
      in favor of seller, payable monthly at $_____ or more
      including interest at _____ %
      ☐ fixed rate   ☐ other _____
      all due ☐_____ years from date of origination or ☐ upon sale or
      transfer of the property.
      A late charge of $_____ shall be due on any installment not paid
      within _____ days of the date due.
      Additional terms: _____
      _____.

   H. **NEW SECOND LOAN** - Buyer to apply for, qualify for, and obtain new
      second loan in the amount of .... $_____
      payable monthly at approximately $_____
      including interest at origination not to exceed _____ %
      ☐ fixed rate   ☐ other _____
      all due _____ years from date of origination.
      Buyer's loan fees not to exceed $_____ .
      Seller agrees to pay a maximum of _____ FHA/VA discount points.
      Additional terms:_____
      _____.

   I. **EXISTING SECOND LOAN** - Buyer to ☐ assume ☐ take title subject
      to an existing second loan with an approximate balance of .... $_____
      payable monthly at $_____ including interest at _____ %
      ☐ fixed rate   ☐ other _____
      Buyers loan fees not to exceed $_____ .
      Additional terms:_____
      _____.

   J. **OTHER PROVISIONS** - If buyer assumes or takes title "subject to" an existing
      loan, seller shall provide buyer with copies of applicable notes and trust deeds.
      Buyer is allowed _____ calendar days after receipt of such copies to
      examine the copies for the features that affect the loan and to notify seller in
      writing of disapproval. Buyer shall not unreasonably withhold approval.
      Failure to notify seller in writing shall conclusively be considered approval.

   K. **ADDITIONAL FINANCING TERMS:** _____
      _____
      _____

   L. TOTAL PURCHASE PRICE.. $_____

(continued)

Buyer and seller acknowledge receiving a duplicate of this page, which is page 3 of ____ pages.
        Buyers' initials (_____) (_____)   Sellers' initials (_____) (_____)

PURCHASE CONTRACT FOR REAL ESTATE AND DEPOSIT RECEIPT

Property known as _____

11. TITLE: Title is to be free of conditions, easements, encumbrances, liens, restrictions, and rights of record other than the following:
   A. Current property taxes;
   B. Covenants, conditions, restrictions, and public utility easements of record, if any, if the items do not adversely affect the continuing use of the property for the purposes for which it is currently used, unless the buyer reasonably disapproves in writing within _____ calendar days of receipt of a current preliminary report furnished at _____ expense; and
   C. Seller shall furnish buyer at _____ expense, a _____ policy issued by _____ company, showing title vested in buyer subject only to the above. If seller is unwilling or unable to eliminate any title matter disapproved by buyer as indicated above, the buyer may end this agreement. If seller fails to deliver title as indicated above, buyer may end this agreement. In either case, deposit shall be returned to the buyer.

12. VESTING: The title shall vest as follows: _____
_____ unless noted otherwise in the buyer's escrow instructions.

13. PRORATIONS: Association dues, interest, payments on assessments and bonds assumed by the buyer, premiums on insurance acceptable to the buyer, property taxes, rents, and _____
_____ shall be paid current and prorated as of
☐ the day the deed records; or ☐ _____.
Bonds or assessments that are now a lien shall be paid current by seller; payments not yet due to be
☐ assumed by the buyer, ☐ paid in full by the seller, including payments not yet due; or
☐ _____.
County transfer tax, if applicable, shall be paid by _____ . The _____
transfer tax or transfer fee shall be paid by _____ . Reassessment of the property when ownership changes affects taxes to be paid. A supplemental tax bill may be issued, which shall be paid by the seller for periods before escrow closes and by the buyer for periods after escrow closes. Buyer and seller shall handle between themselves tax bills issued after escrow closes.

14. TAX WITHHOLDING: Under the Foreign Investment in Real Property Tax Act (FIRPTA), buyers of U.S. real property *must* deduct and withhold from the seller's proceeds 10% of the gross sales price unless an exemption applies. States may require that additional money be withheld.

15. OTHER TERMS AND CONDITIONS:
_____
_____
_____
_____
_____
_____

16. ATTORNEY'S FEES: In any action, arbitration, or proceeding arising out of this agreement, the prevailing party shall be entitled to reasonable attorney's fees and costs.

(continued)

Buyer and seller acknowledge receiving a duplicate of this page, which is page 4 of ____ pages.
       Buyers' initials (_____) (_____)   Sellers' initials (_____) (_____)

PURCHASE CONTRACT FOR REAL ESTATE AND DEPOSIT RECEIPT

Property known as _____

17. ENTIRE CONTRACT:
  A. Time is important.
  B. All earlier agreements between buyer and seller are made a part of this agreement, which makes up the whole contract. The terms of this contract are intended by buyer and seller as their final agreement about the terms that are included in this contract. The terms of this contract may not be contradicted by evidence of any earlier agreement or any oral contract made at the same time as this written contract.
  C. The buyer and seller agree that this contract makes up the complete and exclusive statement of the contract's terms and that no extraneous evidence of any kind may be introduced in any judicial or arbitration proceeding, if any, about this contract.

18. AMENDMENTS:
  The buyer and seller may not alter, amend, change, or modify this contract except by further agreement in writing signed by both buyer and seller.

19. OFFER:
  A. This makes up an offer to purchase the property described.
  B. Unless acceptance is signed by seller and a signed copy is delivered in person, by mail, or facsimile and received by the buyer at the address indicated below within _____ calendar days of the date of this contract, this offer will be considered revoked and the deposit shall be returned.
  C. Buyer has read and acknowledges receipt of a copy of this offer.
  D. This agreement and any addition or modification relating to this agreement including any photocopy or facsimile of this contract may be signed in two or more counterparts, all of which shall make up one and the same writing.

BUYER:_____   BUYER:_____
Address:_____   Address:_____
_____   _____
Telephone:_____   Telephone:_____

ACCEPTANCE

The seller who signed below accepts and agrees to sell the property in the manner indicated below.
  ☐ On the above terms and conditions.   ☐ Subject to the attached counteroffer.

SELLER:_____   SELLER:_____
Address:_____   Address:_____
_____   _____
Telephone:_____   Telephone:_____

Buyer and Seller acknowledge receiving a duplicate of this page, which is page 5 of ____ pages.
Buyers' initials (_____) (_____)   Sellers' initials (_____) (_____)

PURCHASE CONTRACT FOR REAL ESTATE
ADDITIONAL TERMS AND CONDITIONS
This is meant to be a legally binding agreement. Read it carefully.

This document contains additional terms and conditions to the Purchase Contract for Real Estate and Deposit Receipt for the purchase of the property located in the state of_____,
county of _____, city of _____,
and known as _____
This document, when used, is meant to be an addition to the Purchase Contract for Real Estate and Deposit Receipt.

CAPTIONS: The headings and captions in this document are to make reference easy and are not intended as a part of this agreement.

To be included in the agreement, items *must* be initialed by both *buyer(s)* and *seller(s)*.

1. **PHYSICAL AND GEOLOGICAL INSPECTIONS:**
    A. Buyer has the right, at buyer's expense, to select a licensed contractor and /or other qualified professional(s) to make inspections of the property for possible environmental hazards.
        * These inspections can include inspections, investigations, tests, and other studies.
        * The inspections can include but are not limited to the fixtures and fittings of the property and controls for the fixtures and fittings, if any; geological conditions; and possible environmental hazards including substances, products, and other conditions.
    B. Buyer shall keep the property free and clear of any liens. Buyer shall indemnify and hold seller harmless from all liability, claims, demands, damages, or costs and shall repair all damages to the property arising from the inspections.
    C. Buyer shall make all claims about defects in the condition of the property that adversely affect continuing use of the property for the purposes for which it is currently being used or as _____ in writing, supported by written reports, if any. The buyer shall cause these documents to be delivered to the seller, within the number of calendar days specified below of the acceptance of the offer. For all types of physical inspections, except geological inspections, the documents shall be delivered within _____ calendar days. For geological inspections the documents shall be delivered within _____ calendar days.
    D. Buyer shall provide seller with copies, at no cost to the seller, of all reports about the property obtained by the buyer.
    E. Buyer may cancel this agreement if any of these reports disclose conditions or information unacceptable to the buyer, which the seller is unable or unwilling to correct.
    F. Seller shall make the property available for all inspections.
    G. *Buyer's failure to notify seller in writing regarding the above shall conclusively be considered approval.*
        Initials: Buyers: _____   _____   Sellers: _____   _____
                                                                                (continued)

Buyer and seller acknowledge receiving a duplicate of this page, which is page 1 of ____ pages.
        Buyers' initials (_____) (_____)   Sellers' initials (_____) (_____)

PURCHASE CONTRACT FOR REAL ESTATE
ADDITIONAL TERMS AND CONDITIONS

Property known as _____

2. PEST CONTROL

A. Within _____ calendar days of acceptance of the offer, seller shall furnish buyer, at the expense of ☐ buyer, ☐ seller, a current written report of an inspection by _____ _____, a licensed pest control operator. This inspection shall be of one or more of the following areas: ☐ the main building, ☐ detached garage(s) or carport(s), if any, and ☐ the following other structure(s) on the property:_____ _____.

B. If either Buyer or Seller request it, the report shall separately identify each recommendation for corrective action as follows:
Type 1: Infestation or infection that is evident.
Type 2: Conditions present that are considered likely to lead to infestation or infection.

C. If no infestation or infection by wood-destroying pests or organisms is found, the report shall include a written certification that on the inspection date no evidence of active infestation or infection was found.

D. All work recommended to correct conditions described as type 1 shall be at the expense of the ☐ seller. ☐ buyer.

E. All work recommended to correct conditions described as type 2, if requested by the buyer, shall be at the expense of the ☐ seller. ☐ buyer.

F. The repairs shall be done with good workmanship and materials of comparable quality to the originals. These repairs shall include repairs and the replacement of materials removed for repairs. Buyer and seller understand that exact restoration of appearance or cosmetic items following all such repairs is not included.

G. Funds for work agreed to be performed after escrow closes shall be held in escrow and paid on receipt of written certification that the inspected property is now free of active infestation or infection.

H. If the report recommends inspection of inaccessible areas, buyer has the option to accept and approve the report, or within _____ calendar days from receipt of the report to request in writing that a further inspection be made. *Buyer's failure to notify seller in writing of such request shall conclusively be considered approval of the report.*
If additional inspection recommends type 1 or 2 corrective measures, such work shall be done at the expense of whoever is designated in section 2D and/or 2E above. If no infestation is found, the cost of inspection, entry, and closing of inaccessible areas shall be at buyer's expense.

I. Other _____
_____
_____
_____
_____

Initials: Buyers: _____   _____   Sellers: _____   _____

(continued)

Buyer and seller acknowledge receiving a duplicate of this page, which is page 2 of ____ pages.
Buyers' initials (_____) (_____)   Sellers' initials (_____) (_____)

PURCHASE CONTRACT FOR REAL ESTATE
ADDITIONAL TERMS AND CONDITIONS

Property known as _____

3. ENERGY CONSERVATION RETROFIT:

If applicable, governmental laws require that the property be made to conform to minimum energy conservation standards as a condition of sale or transfer; ☐ buyer, ☐ seller shall comply with and pay for the work necessary to meet these requirements. If the seller must bring the property into compliance, the seller may, where the law permits, authorize escrow to credit the buyer with enough funds to cover the cost of the retrofit.

    Initials: Buyers: _____ _____   Sellers: _____ _____

4. FLOOD HAZARD AREA DISCLOSURE:

The buyer is informed that the property is located in a "Special Flood Hazard Area" as set forth on a Federal Emergency Management Agency (FEMA) "Flood Insurance Rate Map" (FIRM) or "Flood Hazard Boundary Map" (FHBM).

  A. The law requires that, to obtain financing on most structures located in a "Special Flood Hazard Area," lenders require flood insurance where the property or its attachments are security for a loan.

  B. No representation is made by the seller as to the legal or economic effects of the National Flood Insurance Program and related legislation.

    Initials: Buyers: _____ _____   Sellers: _____ _____

5. HOME PROTECTION PLAN:

Home protection plans may provide additional protection and benefit to seller and buyer. The buyer and seller agree to include a home protection plan to be issued by _____

_____

at a cost not to exceed $_____ to be paid for by ☐ Buyer, ☐ Seller.

    Initials: Buyers: _____ _____   Sellers: _____ _____

6. CONDOMINIUM/PLANNED UNIT DEVELOPMENT (PUD):

  A. The property is a ☐ condominium ☐ planned unit development (PUD) designated as unit _____ and _____ parking spaces, and an undivided interest in community areas, and

_____.

The current monthly assessment charge, fees, or dues by the homeowner's association or other governing body is $_____.

  B. As soon as practical, seller shall provide buyer with copies of any documents required by law including the articles of incorporation; claims; covenants, conditions, and restrictions; current rules and regulations; litigations; most current financial statement; and pending special assessments.

  C. Buyer is allowed _____ calendar days from receipt to review these documents. If documents disclose conditions or information unacceptable to buyer, buyer may cancel this agreement.

  D. *Buyer's failure to notify seller in writing shall conclusively be considered approval.*

    Initials: Buyers: _____ _____   Sellers: _____ _____

                                                         (continued)

Buyer and seller acknowledge receiving a duplicate of this page, which is page 3 of _____ pages.

    Buyers' initials (_____) (_____)   Sellers' initials (_____) (_____)

PURCHASE CONTRACT FOR REAL ESTATE
ADDITIONAL TERMS AND CONDITIONS

Property known as _____

7. **LIQUIDATED DAMAGES:** If buyer fails to complete purchase of the property because of any default of the buyer, seller is released from obligation to sell the property to buyer. Seller may then proceed against buyer on any claim or remedy that seller may have in equity or law. By initialing this paragraph, buyer and seller agree that seller shall retain the deposit as liquidated damages.
   NOTICE: Funds deposited in trust accounts or in escrow are not released automatically in the event of a dispute. Release of funds requires written agreement of the parties, judicial decision, or arbitration.

    Initials: Buyers: _____ _____   Sellers: _____ _____

8. **DISPUTE ARBITRATION:** Any dispute or claim in law or equity arising out of this contract or any resulting transaction shall be decided by neutral binding arbitration in accordance with the rules of the American Arbitration Association and not by state law except as the law provides for judicial review of arbitration proceedings. Judgment upon the award rendered by the arbitrator shall be entered in any court having jurisdiction over the case. The parties shall have the right of discovery.
   The following matters are excluded from arbitration:
   A. A judicial or nonjudicial foreclosure or other action or proceeding to enforce a deed of trust, mortgage, or a real property sales contract.
   B. An unlawful detainer action.
   C. The filing or enforcement of a mechanic's lien.
   D. Any matter that is within the jurisdiction of a probate court, and/or
   E. Bodily injury, wrongful death, hidden or evident defects, and actions to which civil codes apply. The filing of a judicial action to enable the recording of a notice of pending action, for order of attachment, receivership, injunction, or other temporary remedies, shall not be a waiver of the right to arbitrate under this provision.
   NOTICE: Agreement to this provision is voluntary. If you refuse to submit to arbitration after agreeing to this provision, you may be forced to arbitrate. By initialing below you are
   A. Agreeing to have any dispute arising out of the matters included in this "Dispute Arbitration" provision decided by neutral arbitration as provided by your state law.
   B. Giving up any rights you may possess to have the dispute litigated in a court or jury trial.
   C. Giving up your judicial rights to discovery and appeal, unless those rights are specifically included in the "Dispute Arbitration" provision.
   We have read and understood this provision to arbitrate a dispute, and we agree to this provision.

    Initials: Buyers: _____ _____   Sellers: _____ _____

Receipt of this document is acknowledged:
Date:_____   Seller: _____
Date:_____   Seller: _____
Date:_____   Buyer: _____
Date:_____   Buyer: _____

Buyer and seller acknowledge receiving a duplicate of this page, which is page 4 of ____ pages.
    Buyers' initials (_____) (_____)   Sellers' initials (_____) (_____)

CONTRACT CHANGES AND ADDITIONS

This is meant to be a legally binding agreement. Read it carefully.

The following changes and additions are united with and made a part of the Purchase Contract for Real Estate and Deposit Receipt that is dated _____

between _____ , the seller, and

_____ , the buyer, on the property

known as _____ .

The changes and additions are as follows:

_____
_____
_____
_____
_____
_____
_____
_____
_____
_____
_____
_____
_____
_____
_____
_____
_____
_____
_____
_____
_____
_____
_____
_____

Receipt of this notice is acknowledged:

Date:_____   Seller:_____
Date:_____   Seller:_____
Date:_____   Buyer:_____
Date:_____   Buyer:_____

Buyer and seller acknowledge receiving a duplicate of this page, which is page ____ of ____ pages.
Buyers' initials (_____) (_____)   Sellers' initials (_____) (_____)

COUNTEROFFER

This is meant to be a legally binding agreement. Read it carefully.

This counteroffer to the Purchase Contract for Real Estate and Deposit Receipt on the property known as _____ is dated _____. In this contract _____ is referred to as the buyer and _____ is referred to as the seller.

Seller accepts all of the conditions and terms in the agreement noted above with the following changes:

_____

_____

_____

_____

_____

_____

_____

_____

_____

_____

_____

_____

_____

_____

_____

_____

_____

_____

The seller retains the right to continue to offer the property described for sale. The seller also retains the right to agree to any offer acceptable to seller at any time before the personal acceptance by seller of a copy of this counteroffer, properly accepted and signed by the buyer. *Accept* as used in this document, includes delivery in person, by mail, or by facsimile.

If this counteroffer is not accepted on or before the date of _____ at _____ A.M./P.M., the counteroffer shall be considered canceled and the deposit shall be returned to the buyer. The seller's agreement to another offer shall cancel this counteroffer. This counteroffer and any addition or modification relating to it, including any photocopy or facsimile of it, may be signed in two or more duplicates, all of which will make up the same writing. Acceptance of a copy is acknowledged.

Date: _____   Seller: _____

Time: _____   Seller: _____

(continued)

Buyer and seller acknowledge receiving a duplicate of this page, which is page 1 of ____ pages.
Buyers' initials (_____) (_____)   Sellers' initials (_____) (_____)

COUNTEROFFER

This is meant to be a legally binding agreement. Read it carefully.

Property known as _____

☐ The undersigned buyer accepts the above counteroffer without addition or modification, OR
☐ The undersigned buyer accepts the above counteroffer with the following additions or modifications:

If the following additions or modifications are not accepted and a copy properly accepted and signed is not personally delivered to the buyer or _____, the agent obtaining the offer, on or before _____ at _____ A.M./P.M., the counteroffer shall be considered canceled and the deposit shall be returned to the buyer. Acceptance of a copy is acknowledged.

_____
_____
_____
_____
_____
_____
_____
_____
_____
_____

Date:_____   Buyer:_____
Time:_____   Buyer:_____

Acceptance of a signed copy on_____ at _____ A.M./P.M. by seller is acknowledged.

IF BUYER MADE ADDITIONS OR MODIFICATIONS ABOVE, THE FOLLOWING IS REQUIRED:
Seller accepts buyer's additions or modifications to seller's counteroffer. The seller agrees to sell on the above terms and conditions. Seller acknowledges receipt of a copy.

Date:_____   Seller:_____
Time:_____   Seller:_____

Buyer and seller acknowledge receiving a duplicate of this page, which is page 2 of ____ pages.
           Buyers' initials (_____) (_____)   Sellers' initials (_____) (_____)

CONDITION(S) RELEASE
This is meant to be a legally binding agreement. Read it carefully.

This addition is a part of the Purchase Contract for Real Estate and Deposit Receipt that is dated
_____between _____(seller)
and _____(buyer) on the property known as
_____ .

Seller has the right to continue to offer subject property for sale.

If the seller accepts a later written offer, in accordance with the named buyer's rights, the buyer shall
have _____hours _____days following receiving notice to remove and renounce in writing the
following condition(s): _____
_____
_____
_____
_____
_____
_____

In the event buyer shall fail to remove the condition(s) within the above time limit, the Purchase Contract
for Real Estate and Deposit Receipt and this agreement shall end and become voidable and the buyer's
deposit shall be returned to the buyer.

This Condition(s) Release shall be considered to have been received by buyer when buyer, or buyer's
agent, has received notice by delivery in person or by certified mail addressed to _____
_____ .

If notice is given by mail, the buyer has until 6:00 P.M. of the third day following the date of mailing
(unless the notice provides another time) to deliver to the seller the buyer's written agreement to remove
and void the condition(s).

The person or persons signing below acknowledge receiving a copy of this document.

RECEIPT FOR DELIVERY IN PERSON

Date:_____   Seller:_____
Date:_____   Seller:_____

Date:_____   Buyer:_____
Date:_____   Buyer:_____

Buyer and seller acknowledge receiving a duplicate of this page, which is page 1 of ____ pages.
     Buyers' initials (_____) (_____)   Sellers' initials (_____) (_____)

ASSIGNMENT OF CONTRACT

Date: _____

Owner: _____   Original Buyer: _____

Address: _____   Address: _____
_____   _____

Telephone: _____   Telephone: _____
Fax Line: _____   Fax Line: _____
Cell Line: _____   Cell Line: _____
E-Mail: _____   E-Mail: _____

New Buyer: _____

Address: _____
_____

Telephone: _____

Fax line: _____

Cell Line: _____

E-mail: _____

Contract Date: _____

Property Address: _____
_____

_____ (Original Buyer) hereby exercises their unquali ed right to assign all their rights, obligations, and responsibilities in the above noted Contract dated _____, with _____ (Owner) to _____ (New Buyer). The new buyer of this property hereby agrees to ful ll all of the same terms and conditions of the above referenced Contract, including all closing requirements as originally stated.

The total consideration for this Assignment payable from the New Buyer to the Original Buyer shall be: _____ dollars ($), payable at _____ in the form of a Cashier's check as of the date of the execution of this Assignment of Contract.

Original Buyer: _____   New Buyer: _____
_____   _____
Date: _____   Date: _____

PROMISSORY NOTES

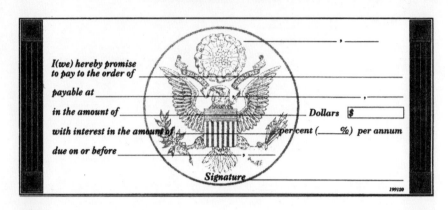

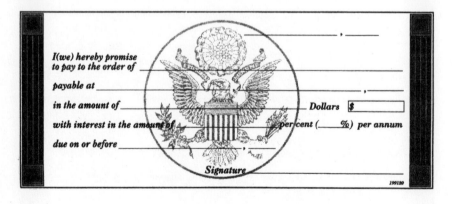

GLOSSARY

Abatement notice   A notice to decrease or cease an illegal or unreasonable irritant that hurts, hinders, or damages others or creates a repeated or persisting interference with another's right.

Abstract of title   A summary of the history of ownership of a property from public records. This history includes all changes of ownership and claims against the property.

Acceleration clause   A provision in a loan document that makes the balance owed on a loan due and payable immediately after a specified event occurs. The event may be missing a payment or violating another provision of the loan.

Acknowledgment   A formal declaration before a public official that one has signed a specific document.

Adjustable rate loan   Adjustable rate mortgage, ARM; a loan that allows adjustments in the interest rate at specified times based on a named index.

Adjustable rate mortgage   *See* Adjustable rate loan.

Adjusted basis   The original cost plus capital improvements minus depreciation. Use adjusted basis to compute taxable gain or loss on the sale of a home.

Adjusted sales price   As a seller, the price for which you sell your home minus closing costs and commission, if applicable.

Agent   A person authorized by another, the principal, to act for him or her in dealing with third parties.

AITD   *See* All-inclusive trust deed.

Alienation clause   *See* Due-on-sale clause.

All-inclusive trust deed   Wraparound mortgage, AITD; a junior (second, third, and so forth) loan (mortgage or trust deed) at one overall interest rate used to wrap the existing loans into a package. The amount is sufficient to cover the existing loans and provide additional funds for the sellers. Sellers pay on existing loans from buyers' payments. Sellers remain primarily responsible for the original loans.

Amortization   Gradual paying off of the principal on a loan by payment of regular installments of principal and interest.

Annual percentage rate   APR; an interest rate that includes interest, discount points, origination fees, and loan broker's commission.

Appraisal   An examination of a property by a qualified professional to estimate the property's market value as of a specific date.

APR   *See* Annual percentage rate.

Arbitration   Taking of a controversy to an unbiased third person. This person holds a hearing at which both parties may speak and then issues an opinion.

ARM   *See* Adjustable rate loan.

Assessment   Tax or charge by a governmental body for a specific public improvement covering the property owner's portion of costs. Assessments are in addition to normal property taxes.

Assign   Transfer.

Assignee   The person to whom interest is transferred.

Assignment   Transfer of any property to another. Delegation of duties and rights to another.

Assignor   The person from whom interest is transferred.

Assume   Buyers taking over primary responsibility for payment of existing loan. Sellers then become secondarily liable for the loan and for any deficiency judgment.

Assumption fee   Transfer fee; the fee a lender may charge for work involved in allowing buyers to assume primary liability for payment on an existing loan.

Attorney   A person licensed to practice law by giving legal advice or assistance, as well as prosecuting and defending cases in courts.

Authorization to sell   A listing contract allowing a real estate professional to act as an agent in the sale of property. (*See also* Listing.)

Bankruptcy   Relief by a court of an obligation to pay money owed after turning over all property to a court-appointed trustee.

Basis   The cost of a home when purchased, including down payment, loans, and closing costs.

Beneficiary   The lender of money on a property used in a trust deed type of loan.

Beneficiary statement   A statement provided by a lender using a trust deed type of loan that usually lists claims that do not appear on loan documents.

Bill of lading   A contract for the transportation of your goods with a commercial moving company.

Binder   An informal contract listing an agreement's main points, later replaced by a formal, detailed written contract.

Breach of contract   Failure to perform as promised without a legal excuse (a good reason).

Bridge loan   A short-term loan to buyers who are simultaneously selling one house and trying to buy another.

Broker   *See* Real estate broker.

Building codes   Regulations by governments giving requirements and standards for structures built in their jurisdictions.

Building permits   County-issued documents that permit you to build after your plans have been approved by the necessary city and county agencies.

Buyer's agent   Selling agent; a real estate broker or sales associate who represents the buyer in a transaction.

Buyer's broker   A real estate broker who represents the buyer. (*See also* Real estate broker.)

Buyer's fees   Charges that are paid for by the buyers.

Buyer's market   A condition in which there are more sellers than buyers; prices generally decrease.

Call   Demand payment of a debt.

Capital asset   Property, both real and personal, held by a taxpayer and not excluded by tax laws.

Capital gain   Profit from selling or exchanging a capital asset in excess of the cost.

Capital improvements   Additions to property that are permanent, increase property value, and have a useful life of more than one year.

Capitalization rate   The rate of return an investment receives.

Capital loss   Loss from selling or exchanging property other than a personal residence at less than its cost.

Cashier's check   A bank's own check guaranteed to be good by the bank at which it is drawn.

Casualty   Loss of or damage to structures or personal property.

Casualty insurance   *See* Hazard insurance.

CC&Rs   Covenants, conditions, and restrictions; a document listing private restrictions on property. Often used when buyers have an interest in common areas.

Certificate of title   A report, produced by a party providing abstracts of titles, stating that based on an examination of public records, the title is properly vested in the present owner.

Classified advertisements   Advertisements that are separated by type and listed accordingly.

Closing   Closing escrow, settlement; the final phase of a real estate transaction that involves signing loan documents, paying closing costs, and delivering the deed. (*See also* Escrow.)

Closing costs   Costs of sale; the additional expenses over and above the purchase price of buying and selling real estate.

Closing escrow   *See* Closing.

Closing fee   *See* Closing.

Closing statement   A written, itemized account given to both sellers and buyers at closing by the escrow holder and detailing receipts, disbursements, charges, credits, and prorations.

Commission   Payments to an agent, such as a real estate broker, for services in the selling or buying of a home.

Commitment   An oral or written agreement to make a loan made by a lender to a potential buyer.

Competent person   A person who meets certain criteria set by a state for competency. These laws often include being a natural person who is an adult or an emancipated minor, mentally competent, and not a felon deprived of civil rights; an artificial person may also meet the requirements.

Completion bond   A bond ensuring that if a contractor does not complete a project, an insurance company will pay for the remaining work to be done.

Completion notice   Copy of the document you file and record with your county when work on your home is complete; it places time limits for mechanics' liens.

Condemnation   The act of taking private property for public use after payment of a fair price (compensation).

Conditions   Requirements that must precede the performance or effectiveness of something else. Provisions or qualifications in a deed that if violated or not performed nullify the deed.

Condominium   An undivided ownership in common in a portion of a piece of real property plus a separate interest in space in a building.

Consideration   Anything of value that influences a person to enter into a contract including money, a deed, an item of personal property, an act (including the payment of money), a service, or a promise (such as to pay on a loan). Acts or services must be performed after you and the buyers enter into the contract.

Contingency   A condition on which a valid contract depends.

Contingency release   Wipe-out clause, kick-out provision; provisions providing that you will continue to market your home until you receive another offer to purchase your home that does not contain the contingencies you indicated or buyers remove those contingencies you specified. After you receive a contract without the detailed contingencies, the original buyers have the specified time you agreed on to remove the contingencies or you may sell your home to the buyers who offered you a contract without the contingencies.

Contract for deed   *See* Land sales contract.

Controller's deed   *See* Tax deed.

Conventional loan   A loan that is not guaranteed or insured by a government agency.

Convey   Transfer.

Costs of sale   *See* Closing costs.

Counteroffer   A statement by a person to whom an offer is made proposing a new offer to the original offeror.

Counterparts   Two documents considered as one.

Covenants   Agreements or promises contained in and conveyed by a deed that are inseparable from the property; pledges for the performance or nonperformance of certain acts or the use or nonuse of property.

Cram-down provision   *See* Short-sale provision.

Credit report   A detailed report of a person's credit history and rating.

Dedication   A giving of land by a property owner to the public for public use.

Deed   A document containing a detailed written description of the property that transfers property ownership.

Deed of trust   *See* Trust deed.

Default   Failure of a person to fulfill an obligation or perform a duty; failure to make a loan payment when it is due.

Default insurance   *See* Mortgage default insurance.

Deficiency judgment   A court decision making an individual personally liable for payoff of a remaining amount due because the full amount was not obtained by foreclosure.

Delinquent payment   A payment that was not paid when it was due.

Demand fee   Demand for payoff charge; a fee for a written request to a lender for lender's demand for payment of the loan in full and the supporting documents necessary for release of the lien against the property.

Demand for payoff charge   *See* Demand fee.

Deposit   Money that buyers submit with a purchase offer as evidence of their intention and ability to buy.

Depreciation   Loss in value from any cause.

Disclosure   Making known things that were previously unknown.

Discount points   *See* Points.

Discovery   Disclosure of things previously unknown.

Discrimination   Giving or withholding particular advantages to or from certain types of persons arbitrarily selected from a larger group. Treating other persons unfairly or denying them normal privileges.

Display advertisements   Large advertisements that often contain illustrations.

Divided agency   Agent's action in representing both parties in a transaction without the knowledge and consent of both.

Documentary transfer tax   *See* Transfer tax.

Down payment   Money that you and buyers agree on, or that a lender requires, that buyers pay toward the purchase price before escrow can close.

Drawing deed fee   A fee for the preparation of a deed.

Dual agent   A broker acting either directly, or through an associate licensee, as agent for both seller and buyer.

Due-on-sale clause   Alienation clause; an acceleration clause in a loan giving the lender the right to demand all sums owed due at once and payable if the property owner transfers title.

Earnest money   *See* Deposit.

Easement   The right a property owner has to use the land of another for a special purpose. It may be valid even if unidentified, unlocated, unmentioned, and unrecorded.

Emancipated minor   A person who is under the age to legally be an adult in the state in which they live but who has some other criteria that allow them to function as adults. The criteria may include being lawfully married or divorced, on duty in the armed forces, or emancipated by court order.

Eminent domain   Governments' power that allows them to take private property for public use after paying what they feel to be a fair price.

Encumbrance   A charge, claim, or lien against a property or personal right or interest in a property that affects or limits the title but does not prevent transfer.

Equity   The part of a property's current value that is owned and on which no money is owed; the property's value minus the liens owed against the property.

Escrow   A process in the transfer of real property in which buyers and sellers deposit documents or money with a neutral third party (the escrow holder). Buyers and sellers give instructions to the escrow holder to hold and deliver documents and money if certain conditions are met.

Escrow instructions   A written agreement between sellers and buyers that extrapolates the purchase contract into a form used as directions on how to conduct and close the escrow.

Exclusive agency listing   A listing with only one agency that provides that if the real estate professional obtains the buyer, you must pay the broker the commission. If you sell your home yourself, you are not liable for the commission.

Exclusive right to sell listing   A listing providing that, during the time listed, only that broker has the right to sell your home and earn the commission no matter who makes the sale.

Extended coverage title insurance   This coverage protects against numerous risks that are not a matter of record.

FHA   Federal Housing Administration; a federal governmental agency that manages FHA-insured loans to protect lenders in case of default by buyers.

FHA loan   Financing by having a conventional loan made by a lender and insured by the Federal Housing Administration.

Fiduciary   A person who is in a position of trust who must act in the best interest of clients.

Fire insurance   *See* Hazard insurance.

Fixed-rate loan   A loan on which the percentage of interest remains at the same rate over the life of the loan. The payments of principal remain equal during the entire period.

Fixture   Items permanently attached to or for which special openings were made in a home and its associated structures.

Fix-up costs   The expenses of improvements, repairs, and attractiveness items.

Flood Hazard Area Disclosure   A federally required disclosure to inform buyers that the property is located in a region designated as a special flood hazard area.

Flyers   Leaflets for mass distribution.

Foreclosure   The process by which a property on which a borrower has not paid is sold to satisfy a loan against the property.

Fraud   Willfully concealing or misrepresenting a material fact in order to influence another person to take action. The action results in the person's loss of property or legal rights.

FSBO   For sale by owner; a phrase describing a homeowner selling property without using a real estate broker.

Geological inspection   Inspection for potential or actual geological problems, as well as examination of records to determine whether property falls within any special zones.

Gift deed   A deed given for love and affection.

GI loan   *See* VA loan.

Grant deed   A deed using the word *grant* in the clause that transfers ownership.

Grantee   Buyer; receiver of a title to a property.

Grantor   Seller; holder of a title to a property.

Gross income   Total income it is possible to receive before operating expenses.

Guarantee of title   A warranty that title is vested in the party shown on the deed.

Hazard insurance   Casualty insurance, fire insurance; insurance protection against stated specific hazards such as fire, hail, windstorms, earthquakes, floods, civil disturbances, explosions, riots, theft, and vandalism.

Home equity line of credit   Credit given by a lender based on the amount of one's equity in a property. The line of credit becomes a loan secured by a mortgage or trust deed when the borrower uses some or all of the credit.

Home inspection   *See* Physical inspection.

Home inspector   A qualified person who examines and reports on the general condition of a home's site and structures.

Homeowner's association dues Monthly fees owners of homes pay to their home-owner's association for the items it provides.

Homeowner's insurance A policy protecting a homeowner from liability and casu-alty hazards listed in the policy. (*See also* Hazard insurance.)

Home protection plan *See* Home warranty.

Home warranty Home protection plan; insurance that items listed are in working order for the specified length of time.

Impounds Reserve fund; funds held by the lender to assure payment in the future of recurring expenses. These expenses can include insurance premiums and taxes.

Improper delivery Delivery of a deed that has not passed out of seller's control and/or was not delivered to buyers during the seller's lifetime.

Improvement costs Expenses for permanent additions.

Improvement notices Documents sent by governments giving notice of one-time charges for planned improvements (e.g., sidewalks).

Imputed interest rate The minimum rate the IRS requires for a seller-financed loan. If you charge less than the minimum rate the IRS taxes you on the minimum.

Index A measurement of interest rates on which changes in interest charges on adjust-able rate loans are based.

Inspection records Notices indicating that inspections have been conducted by the proper local authorities at certain specified points in the building process.

Inspection reports Reports by inspectors about the condition of various aspects of your property, including defects and repairs considered necessary.

Installment note A loan paid back in at least two payments of principal on different dates.

Installment sale A sale that allows the seller to receive payments in more than one tax year.

Interest A charge or rate paid in arrears (after incurred) to a lender for borrowing money.

Interest-only loan A loan for which only the interest is paid and no principal is repaid until the final installment.

Interpleader action Request by a closing agent or escrow holder that a court take custody of the deposited funds and make a judgment as to their distribution.

Jointly and severally liable Liable along with other parties and personally liable.

Joint tenancy Vesting wherein two or more parties acquire title at the same time. Each party has an equal, undivided interest and equal right to possess the property, including automatic right of survivorship.

Judgment Final determination by a court of a matter presented to it. A general mon-etary obligation on all property of the person who owes the money. This obligation applies in each county where an abstract of the court judgment was recorded.

Kick-out provision   *See* Contingency release.

Lack of capacity   Inability to enter into a contract because one is not a competent person by his or her state's criteria.

Landfill   Soil moved onto the site from another location.

Landlord   The owner or lessor of real property.

Land sales contract   Contract for deed, real property sales contract; an agreement in which the seller retains title to property until the buyer performs all contract conditions.

Lease   A contract that transfers possession and use of designated property for a limited, stated time under specified conditions.

Lease option   A contract that stipulates that potential buyers are leasing a property for an agreed-on rental payment. These buyers have the right to purchase the property before the specified future date for the amount listed in the contract. Part of the lease payment is considered option money toward the purchase price.

Lease purchase   A contract that states that buyers are leasing the property for the agreed-on amount and conditions. The buyers agree to purchase the property at the agreed-on time for the agreed-on amount.

Legal description   A formal description giving a property's location, size, and boundaries in written and/or map form.

Lessee   The tenant or person who leases property from the landlord in order to use it.

Lessor   The landlord or owner of property who leases the property to the tenant for the tenant's use.

Liability   Responsibility for damages to other people or property; what you owe against an asset.

Lien   A claim against a property making the property security for debts such as loans, mechanic's liens, and taxes.

Lien releases   Documents releasing one from monetary liability to the party listed after fully paying that party.

Liquidated damages   The amount of money you may keep if the buyers default or breach the contact.

Lis pendens   An official recorded notice that legal action is pending against the title to the property.

Listing   Authorization to sell; a contract allowing a real estate broker to act as an agent to buy, lease, or sell property for another.

Litigation   Lawsuits.

Loan disclosure statement   A lender's account summary required by the Federal Truth in Lending Act.

Loan discount fee   *See* Points.

Loan fees   One-time charges by the lender for initiating a loan, including points, appraisal, and credit report on buyers.

Loan origination fee   Lender's charge for arranging and processing a loan, usually based on a percentage of the loan.

Loan tie-in fee   A fee charged by whoever handles closing for their work and liability in conforming to the lender's criteria for the buyers' new loan.

Market value   The amount buyers are willing to pay and sellers are willing to accept within a reasonable time.

Marshal's deed   *See* Sheriff's deed.

Material facts   Any facts that if known would influence a person's decision.

Mechanic's lien   A claim filed against property by a contractor, service provider, or supplier for work done or materials provided for which full payment has not been received.

Median price   The price at which half the properties are more expensive and half the properties are less expensive.

MLS   *See* Multiple Listing Service.

Mortgage   A contract to secure a loan by which you promise your property without giving up possession or title.

Mortgage default insurance   Default insurance; insurance coverage enabling the lender to receive a part of the outstanding balance in the event you default.

Mortgage disability insurance   Insurance coverage enabling you to pay monthly mortgage charges in the event you are totally and permanently disabled.

Mortgagee   Lender of money on property using a mortgage.

Mortgage life insurance   Insurance coverage enabling whomever you designate to pay the loan balance if you die.

Mortgagor   Property owner who borrows money using a mortgage.

Multiple Listing Service   MLS; an agency to which real estate brokers belong in order to pool their listings with other real estate brokers. If a sale is made, the listing and selling brokers share the commission.

Negative amortization   Process in which payments on a loan do not cover interest payments and the difference between the payment and interest due are added to the loan balance.

Net listing   A listing providing that the broker retain all money received in excess of the price set by the seller.

Net operating income (NOI)   Gross income minus operating expenses.

Nominal interest rate   Interest rate stated in a promissory note.

Nonconforming uses   Preexisting uses of land allowed to continue even though a current ordinance excluding that use has been enacted for that area.

Notary fee A charge paid to a notary public to witness signatures on some of the legal documents in a transaction.

Notice of default Warning sent to a borrower on a loan cautioning the borrower that the payment is delinquent.

Offset statement A statement regarding a loan provided by the seller when a beneficiary statement is not available.

Open listing A nonexclusive right-to-sell agreement one can make with one or more real estate professionals. It provides that if you sell your home yourself, you are not liable to the broker for a commission. If, however, a real estate professional obtains the buyers for the property, you must pay the broker the commission you have negotiated.

Operating expenses Property taxes, insurance, maintenance, and utilities.

Option A contract to keep an offer to buy, sell, or lease property open for a period and under the agreed-on terms.

Optionee The person who gets the option on a property.

Optionor The owner of a title who gives an option.

Option to buy *See* Purchase option.

Payment records Checks, receipts, and written ledgers.

Payment statements Monthly stubs showing your payment date, amounts applied to principal and interest, and remaining balance due, as well as annual summary statements.

Permission-to-show listing A listing contract that allows a real estate professional to show your property only to the person or persons named in that contract. You pay the commission only if someone on the list purchases your home.

Personal property Items that are not permanently attached to your home or other structures on your property.

Pest control inspection Structural pest control inspection, termite inspection; inspection for infestation or infection by wood-destroying pests or organisms.

Physical inspection Home inspection; examination of the general physical condition of a property's site and structures.

Planned unit development PUD; a subdivision in which the lots are separately owned but other areas are owned in common.

Points Discount points, loan discount fee; a one-time charge by the lender to adjust the yield on the loan to current market conditions or to adjust the rate on the loan to market rate. Each point is equal to 1 percent of the loan balance.

Power of attorney A document that gives one person the power to sign documents for another person.

Power of sale clause   A provision in a loan allowing the lender to foreclose and sell borrower's property publicly without a court procedure.

Preliminary title report   Report summarizing the title search performed by a title company or lawyer for a property.

Prepayment penalty   A fine imposed on a borrower by a lender for the early payoff of a loan or any substantial part of a loan.

Principal   One of the parties in a real estate transaction, either the sellers or the buyers.

Principal residence   An IRS term denoting the residence wherein you spend the most time during the tax year.

Probate court   A court that handles wills and the administration of estates of people who have died.

Promissory note   The written contract you sign promising to pay a definite amount of money by a definite future date.

Property taxes   Taxes; taxes assessed on property at a uniform rate so that the amount of the tax depends on the value.

Property tax statements   Documents that the county assessor's office mails to homeowners itemizing the semiannual or annual tax bill on a home and indicating the payment due dates.

Prorations   Proportional distributions of responsibility for the payment of the expenses of homeownership. This distribution is based on the percentage of an assessment or billing period during which the seller and buyers own the property.

PUD   *See* Planned unit development.

Purchase contract   The contract containing terms and conditions to which you and the buyers agree when you accept the buyers' offer to purchase your home.

Purchase option   Option to buy; the type of contract in which buyers agree to purchase the property for the amount listed in the contract, if they decide to buy your home and make the purchase within the listed period of time, and agree that you keep the option fee if they do not buy the property.

Quitclaim deed   A deed using the word *quitclaim* in the clause granting ownership and thus releasing the grantor from any claim to that property. A quitclaim deed has no warranties.

Real estate   *See* Real property.

Real estate broker   A real estate agent who represents another person in dealing with third parties. This person must take required courses, pass a broker's exam, and be state licensed. A broker may employ other qualified individuals and is responsible for their actions.

Real estate professional   A real estate broker or sales associate.

Real estate sales agent   A person who is licensed by a state and who represents a real estate broker in transactions.

Real Estate Settlement Procedures Act   *See* RESPA.

Real property   Real estate; land and whatever is built on, growing on, or attached to the land.

Real property sales contract   *See* Land sales contract.

Reconveyance deed   A deed that records full satisfaction of a trust deed-secured debt on your property and transfers bare legal title from the trustee to you.

Recording   Official entry of liens, reconveyances, and transactions into the permanent records of a county.

Release of contract   An agreement that all responsibilities and rights occurring as a result of a contract are invalid.

Repair costs   Expenses for work maintaining a home's condition, including replacement and restoration.

Request for notice of default   A recorded notice allowing a county recorder to notify lenders of foreclosure on a property in which the lender has an interest.

Rescind   To cancel a contract and restore the parties to the state they would have been in had the contract never been made.

Reserve fund   *See* Impounds.

RESPA   Real Estate Settlement Procedures Act; a federal law that requires that buyers be given, in advance of closing, information regarding their loan.

Restrictions   Encumbrances that limit the use of real estate by specifying actions the owner must take or cannot take on or with his or her property.

Revocation   Involuntary cancellation that occurs when the time limit has expired and one or both parties do not perform in accordance with the terms of the contract.

Sale leaseback   An agreement in which the seller sells the property to buyers who agree to lease the property back to the seller.

Sales associate   A real estate professional with either a broker's or sales license who acts as an agent for a broker.

Satisfaction of mortgage   A document indicating that you have paid your mortgage off in full.

Seller buy-down loan   A loan in which the effective interest rate is bought down (reduced) during the beginning years of the loan by contributions a seller makes.

Seller carry-back loan   A loan for which the seller acts as a lender to carry back or hold mortgage notes from buyers. These notes may be first, second, or even third loans.

Seller's agent   *See* Listing.

Seller's market   A condition in which there are more buyers than sellers; prices generally increase.

Selling agent   *See* Buyer's agent.

Setback   Laws prohibiting the erection of a building within a certain distance of the curb.

Settlement   *See* Closing.

Settling   Sinking and then coming to rest in one place.

Severalty   Vesting of title in which you hold title by yourself.

Sheriff's deed   Marshal's deed; a deed used by courts in foreclosure or in carrying out a judgment. This deed transfers a debtor's title to a buyer.

Short-sale provision   A lender reducing the amount of the loan payoff.

Single agent   An agent representing only one party in a real estate transaction.

Sliding   The large downward movement of a soil mass out of its previous position.

Slippage   The small downward movement of a soil mass out of its previous position.

Special endorsements   Specific endorsements that modify, expand, or delete the coverage of any insurance policy.

Special Studies Zone Disclosure   A form used to inform buyers that a property is in an area specified as a Special Studies Zone by California law. These zones primarily affect areas where there was or may be serious earthquake destruction.

Specific performance   Law that allows one party to sue another to perform as specified under the terms of their contract.

Standard coverage title insurance   The regular investigation for this insurance generally reveals only matters of record and location of the improvements with respect to the lot line.

Straight note   A promise to pay a loan in which the principal is paid as one lump sum, although the interest may be paid in one lump sum or in installments.

Structural pest control inspection   *See* Pest control inspection.

Subescrow fee   A fee charged by some escrow holders for their costs when they handle money.

Subject-to loan   An existing loan for which buyers take over responsibility for the payments, and seller remains primarily liable in the event of a deficiency judgment.

Survey fee   A fee charged for a survey showing the exact location and boundaries of a property.

Syndication   A form of limited partnership used to make real estate investments.

Take sheet   A form used to collect information necessary to prepare the escrow instructions.

Tax deed   Controller's deed; a deed used by a state to transfer title to the buyers.

Taxes   *See* Property taxes.

Tax parcel number   The number assigned to a piece of property by the local taxing authority.

Tax preparers   Persons who prepare tax returns.

Tax stamps   A method of denoting that a transfer tax has been paid in which stamps are affixed to a deed before the deed may be recorded.

Telephone register   A listing of information regarding telephone calls you receive.

Termination of agency   Ending of an agency agreement.

Termite inspection   *See* Pest control inspection.

Time is of the essence   A statement that one party in a contract must perform certain acts within the stated period before the other party can perform.

Title   Evidence of one's right to a property and the extent of that right.

Title insurance   The policy issued to you by the title company on completion of the final title search protecting against claims in the future based on circumstances in the past.

Title insurance companies   Companies issuing title insurance policies.

Title search   An examination of information recorded on your property at the county recorder's office. This examination verifies that the property has no outstanding claims or liens against it to adversely affect the buyer or lender and that you can transfer clear legal title to the property.

Transfer fee   *See* Assumption fee.

Transfer tax   Documentary transfer tax; a tax that some states allow individual counties or cities to place on the transferring of real property.

Trust deed   A document, used as a security device for the loan on your property, by which you transfer bare (naked) legal title with the power of sale to a trustee. This transfer is in effect until you have totally paid off the loan.

Trustee   A person who holds bare legal title to a property without being the actual owner of the property. The trustee has the power of sale for the lender's benefit.

Trustee's deed   A deed used by a trustee in a foreclosure handled outside of court to transfer the debtor's title to buyers.

Trust funds   Funds held by a closing agent or escrow holder for the benefit of the buyers or seller.

Truth in lending   A federal law that requires disclosure of loan terms to a borrower who is using his or her principal residence as security for a loan.

Unconditional lien release   Waiver of liens; a release, usually signed by a contractor, after a job is complete and you made the final payments waiving and releasing all rights and claims against your home.

Unenforceable   Not able to be enforced; void.

Unlawful detainer   The unjustifiable keeping of possession of real property by someone who originally had the right to possession but no longer has that right.

Unmarketability of title   Inability to sell property because of unacceptable encumbrances and liens on the title.

Usury   Interest charged in excess of what state law permits.

VA   Veterans Administration; the federal government agency that manages VA loans.

VA loan   GI loan; financing made by having a conventional loan made by a lender guaranteed by the Veterans Administration.

Variance   An approved release from current zoning regulations regarding the use or alteration of property.

Vendee   Purchaser or buyer.

Vendor   Owner or seller.

Vesting   Interest that cannot be revoked.

Veterans Administration   *See* VA.

Void   To have no effect; unenforceable at law.

Voidable   Able to be set aside.

Waive   Unilateral voluntary relinquishment of a right of which one is aware.

Waiver of liens   *See* Unconditional lien release.

Walk-through inspection   Buyers' physical examination of a property within a few days before closing verifying that systems, appliances, and the house itself are in the agreed-on condition.

Warranties   Printed or written documents guaranteeing the condition of property or its components.

Warranty deed   A deed in which the grantor explicitly guarantees the title to be as indicated in the deed. The grantor agrees to protect buyers against all claimants to the property.

Wipe-out clause   *See* Contingency release.

Work stoppage clause   A clause in a contract giving a contractor the right to stop work if you do not make the required payments.

Wraparound mortgage   *See* All-inclusive trust deed.

Yield   The return on investment including interest and principal expressed annually.

Zoning   Governmental laws establishing building codes and governing the specific uses of land and buildings.

INDEX